THE REFERENCE SHELF (Continued)

Volume 28

No.
1. Immigration and the United States. Poyntz Tyler. $2.

2. Juvenile Delinquency. G. S. Mc-Clellan. $2.

4. Community Planning. H. L. Marx, Jr. $2.

No.
5. The Government and the Farmer. W. M. Daniels. $2.

6. The Middle East in the Cold War. G. S. McClellan. $2.

Volume 26

No.
5. The Censorship of Books. 2d printing W. M. Daniels. $2.

Volume 24

No.
3. Representative American Speeches: 1951-1952. A. C. Baird. $1.75.

Volume 23

No.
2. Representative American Speeches: 1950-1951. A. C. Baird. $1.75.

Volume 22

No.
3. Representative American Speeches: 1949-1950. A. C. Baird. $1.75.

Volume 20

No.
5. Federal World Government. J. E. Johnsen. $1.50.

THE REFERENCE SHELF

Vol. 32   No. 1

INDIA

Edited by
GRANT S. McCLELLAN
Staff Member, Foreign Policy Association

THE H. W. WILSON COMPANY
NEW YORK   1960

PREFACE

India—the world's most populous democracy—is in dire trouble both at home and abroad. What should America do about India? These are the two outstanding themes of this compilation.

During its twelve years of independence, India, which has followed a neutralist path in foreign policy and claims to be building a democratic society on the "socialist pattern," has been much criticized in this country. Yet in almost the same number of years after independence from British rule, the Indians, like Americans early in our history, have been thrust into internationl problems which are severely testing their early "stand-off" position in world affairs. Now Communist China has made inroads into India's northern frontiers, following its suppression of the revolt in Tibet. As a result many leading Indians have found that the policy of neutrality or nonalignment, as the Indians prefer to call it, in the cold war needs searching reappraisal.

At home India has attempted in its short independent history to begin the march toward economic growth by democratic methods in contrast to its northern neighbors—both the Soviet Union and Communist China—which are seeking the same end by totalitarian methods. Yet India faces serious food shortages in the years immediately ahead, because of its low agricultural productivity and a tremendous population explosion. Lack of capital also impedes its industrial development.

Here lies the interest for the free world in India's experiment —whether it can succeed in raising the standard of living so as to extricate itself from the present production-population dilemma while still retaining democratic institutions. At present most comparative growth statistics show that the draconian methods employed by Communist China are achieving, however inhumanly, greater results.

Most keen observers see in India the challenge of democracy versus dictatorship—a test which may be decisive in the cold war. For if India fails, the example set by Communist China may prove overwhelmingly attractive to other underdeveloped lands in Asia, Africa and Latin America, and to India itself. To many Americans it appears clear that the United States should insure that India succeeds. Walter Lippmann, the distinguished columnist, believes this to be the free world's "glorious gamble" which it must take to preserve freedom. Other Americans are less sure that this country can effectively aid India under its present policies of attempting to achieve economic growth under "socialist planning."

The articles in this compilation, giving both Indian and American views, deal with the many related problems of India's predicament and what, if anything, the United States can do about it. At the outset several articles touching on the Indian historic scene are included. In great part India's present plight arises directly from its deep cultural patterns, as diverse and complex as any nation's in the world.

The editor gratefully expresses his thanks to the various authors and publishers who have granted permission for the use of materials included in this book.

GRANT S. MCCLELLAN

February 1960

CONTENTS

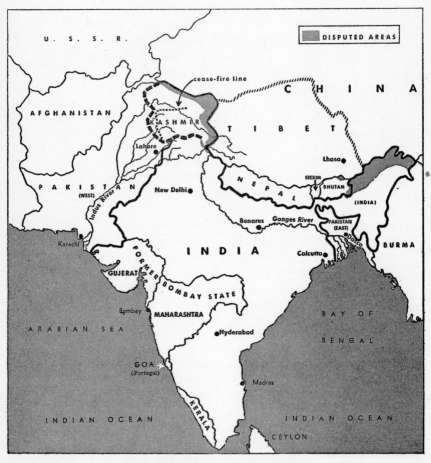

THE INDIAN SUBCONTINENT

Adapted from "Great Decisions. . . 1960." Reprinted by permission of the
Foreign Policy Association.

I. WHAT IS INDIA?

EDITOR'S INTRODUCTION

Many students believe India can hardly be called a nation in the sense that France is. Yet it is an ancient civilization, one of the most complex social and cultural societies known. Its peoples are more varied than those of all Europe and number about the same. Hundreds of languages and various religions and castes divide its people. Many observers fear that in any profound crisis violent chaos or political "balkanization" might ensue. Yet its peoples have risen in the last generation to throw off imperial rule through a nationalist movement now in control of the government which has embarked on a revolution to achieve full nationhood and a welfare society.

The first article in this section briefly points to the salient features of this revolution being undertaken by democratic means —a revolution by consent. The ancient heritage of India and the impact which the period of British rule still exerts on the nation are explained by Vera M. Dean in the next selection. A short discussion of the partition of India and Pakistan follows. Gandhi, who became known and revered throughout the world during the years of India's struggle against British rule, is discussed by India's Prime Minister Jawaharlal Nehru—who is in part the heir to Gandhi's leadership—and by the writer Vincent Sheean. Nehru himself, a complex personality often thought of as a blend between the Orient and the West, is analyzed by the New York *Times* correspondent Robert Trumbull. Brief notes about India's constitution and politics follow, written by Indians —an introduction to present-day India. The facts about the exceedingly high rate of population growth are given last and are included here as being the number one problem with which India must grapple.

REVOLUTION BY CONSENT [1]

Ten years after independence, Jawaharlal Nehru's government in India is facing its most severe test. Outwardly there is simply an economic crisis in which a shortage of capital is holding up development plans, but it is in essence the crisis of democracy in Asia. The question of whether parliamentary democracy can survive in this alien soil will be settled in the next few years, and the stage on which its struggle for survival is to be played out is India. . . .

It would be absurd to expect that in ten years India had created a stable working democracy comparable with that of Britain or the United States. You do not have to be long in India before you see that the government of India does not rest in parliament, or in the cabinet. Nehru alone governs India —just as Winston Churchill governed Britain in 1940-1942. But Nehru (like Churchill) is not a dictator by nature or choice; he pretends that he is in fact as well as in theory the servant of parliament. For him, parliament is an important instrument in carrying out his political and social revolution, which will eventually result in India's becoming a genuine parliamentary democracy. He uses parliament to explain his purposes and plans, to educate the new masters of India, to point the moral that the government of the people is responsible to the people.

Secular, Socialist, Scientific

It is very largely through parliament, which he uses as a sounding board to reach the whole nation, that Nehru has put across a surprisingly clear impression of the nature of the new India he is trying to create. He wants to make India secular, socialist, and scientific, and each concept is in daring opposition to the dead weight of Indian tradition.

By making India secular, Nehru challenges the whole religious structure of Hindu society on which India's way of life has been based for centuries. The Indian constitution's ban on discrimination against the untouchables strikes at the root of religious

[1] From "India's Ten Years of Revolution by Consent," by William Clark, correspondent. *Reporter*. p 15-18. My. 29, '58. Reprinted by permission.

influence on society. The legal, and practical, insistence on equality for Moslems runs counter to that whole trend of history which only ten years ago led to the partitioning of the sub-continent. Yet it is evident that unless India really becomes a secular state, in which a man's religion in no way affects his political status, it will be impossible for the country to be united, democratic, or modern.

The word "socialist," which is often on the lips of the Congress party and of the prime minister, has led to a good deal of misunderstanding abroad, and indeed reflects a muddle in many Indians' minds. . . . Today the most hidebound captains of industry in the Congress party, managers who would expel a trade unionist from their factory, solemnly declare themselves in favor of the "socialist pattern of society." What they seem to mean by this is not public ownership of the means of production but, first, a planned effort to increase production and, second, an effort to smooth out the inequality between wealth and poverty. For Nehru this egalitarianism is a consuming passion. . . .

Perhaps it is in his emphasis on scientific thought as the basis for a new India that Nehru comes most sharply into conflict with the old India. Most Indians just do not accept the relation of scientific cause and effect. . . .

Perhaps it is because eighty per cent of India's food depends on the God-given rains of the monsoon, which may fail or fall out of season, that Indians refuse to equate individual effort with results. Whatever the reason, Nehru has seen that this mentality is a formidable barrier to India's entry into the modern world. . . .

Of course, being scientific means more to India's leaders than just a state of mind. It means having machines instead of mass manpower, veterinary care instead of herds of undernourished diseased cattle, cars instead of bullock carts; it means, in fact, making India an equal partner with its late imperial masters.

What Prospects?

This, then, is the revolution planned by Nehru. In the first ten years of independence enormous strides have been made, most notably in the political sphere. What are the prospects for the next ten years?

They are not so bright. The whole motive power for this basically pro-Western revolution has come from a small group of men who struggled against the British for half their lives and came to respect their adversaries and to admire many of their methods. The "westernizers" in the Congress party are nearly all old men, and are unlikely to provide the leadership for the future. In the next ten years it seems probable that the Congress party will come to be dominated, or at least increasingly influenced, by those who draw their inspiration from Indian tradition and who look to Mahatma Gandhi as the source of political wisdom.

By far the best known of these, and a powerful influence throughout India, is Vinoba Bhave, Gandhi's disciple and now the leader of a movement to solve India's economic problems by charity. He preaches the doctrine that all men are brothers, that the rich should give their surplus land to the poor, and that the villager should grow enough food for himself and his family and devote the rest of his time to handicrafts. He abhors industry. Bhave is not just a lonely crank. He has converted Jayaprakash Narayan, a former leader of the Praja-Socialist party and one of India's best intellects, and many others who are appalled at the difficulties and pitfalls that confront an Asian country trying to enter the industrial race.

These men, honest, self-sacrificing, and devoted, do not wish to concentrate their attention on industrial progress in the Western sense; they would prefer to withdraw from the technological race, which produces Sputniks and atom bombs, and turn their efforts to producing a rural India living in dignified, contented poverty. They are the modern Luddites who, even today, refuse to allow new textile mills to be built, preferring the hundreds of thousands of Gandhian hand looms that pour forth inferior coarse cloth.

Sometimes it seems as if the only alternative to this rather gloomy outlook is Communist rule. Already the Communists have managed to establish themselves as the official opposition to the Congress party in parliament, and . . . [at one time they governed] the state of Kerala. . . . The Communists are well organized, at a time when the Congress organization is breaking down. They have a sense of mission, while Congress has fulfilled its original mission and not yet found another. But the Communists are a small minority and only by the complete failure of the Nehru-Congress régime can they come to power.

The Price of Democracy

If India is to avoid going back to the Middle Ages under the banner of Gandhiism, or forward to 1984 with the Communists, the present policies of the "westernizers" will have to pay off soon. This means that the second Five-Year Plan must make a noticeable impact on the standard of living of the people At the moment that seems unlikely.

The rather modest first Five-Year Plan that ended in 1955 was so successful that Congress political leaders and economic experts were forced to promise something bigger and better for the second plan—which was to be announced shortly before the elections. As a result, an ambitious plan was announced with a very considerable financial gap to be filled by "loans and credits from abroad."

For a time, in 1957, it looked as though these loans and credits were not going to materialize and that the plan would collapse. In desperation, the then Finance Minister T. T. Krishnamachari set off on a tour of the Western capitals, while lesser figures went to Moscow. A substantial loan was arranged in Washington, and Russia made a well-publicized agreement to extend its existing credits at low interest rates.

The plan has been saved from disaster; but it is still cut to the bone, and India's progress has been sadly slowed down. Indeed, the . . . cuts announced at the beginning of May [1958] were so severe that their full impact has been concealed from the Indian people for fear of a serious drop in morale. . . .

It takes capital to industrialize a country, and in a backward country like India capital can only be raised by forced loans from the masses (which is what, in differing ways, Russia did and China is now doing) or by borrowing abroad. If the Indian government were to raise money by squeezing its desperately poor peasants, it could not remain a democracy. The price of democracy is foreign loans, and India's reluctance to request them matches the West's reluctance to grant them.

Even if the loans are forthcoming, it cannot be certain that the plan will succeed in raising living standards significantly. There are two drags on Indian progress that even in favorable circumstances may yet prevent success. One is the political problem of the quarrel with Pakistan, the other the biological problem of "population explosion."

India's Arms Race

. . . Pakistan by claiming the right to create an Islamic state for those Indians who are Moslems, struck at the very root of Nehru's secular-state ideals. . . .

Within the [recent] past, as Pakistan has begun to receive American arms "to defend herself against Russia," India has felt bound to match those deliveries by purchases, mainly from Britain, paid for in cash. The cost is crippling and at present represents the largest single item of foreign-exchange expenditure. As long as the quarrel lasts, both countries will be sadly weakened by it, and there is not much the outside world can do about it. . . .

It is harder to see how anything can be done to solve the population problem in India, a problem that is duplicated in China. But very briefly, the problem is that India's net birth rate has become so high in the past forty years that all the quite considerable increases in production are swallowed up by the new mouths to be fed.

India is already grossly overpopulated, and though it is about one third the size of the United States, it has more than twice the population. The basic cause of Indian (indeed of Asian) poverty is simply that each family has to live on what a single acre of not very fertile ground will produce. Today the government of India spends vast sums of money on propaganda for birth control, but the results are negligible. Still, faith is pinned on the ultimate discovery of a simple contraceptive that can be produced cheaply and taken orally. This, the experts say, will change everything. Non-experts may surely be permitted a wide measure of skepticism.

The chances of success for Nehru's revolution by consent are at best only fair. Yet it seems that it is a gamble well worth the support of the West. The objectives that Nehru's government have set are basically the objectives of the Western world. If it can achieve them, India will certainly become a full partner with the West—prickly and headstrong perhaps, but a living proof to all the world that a backward country can develop itself without giving up its liberties.

We must realize, however, that it does not lie in our power to ensure results; India's future lies in its own hands, not ours, though we may help or hinder. The changes in national outlook and habits which are needed in order to achieve the planned revolution are so great that the verdict of history may well be that such revolutions cannot be achieved by consent. Such a failure would be the knell of democracy in the underdeveloped two thirds of the world.

THE INDIAN-BRITISH HERITAGE [2]

The most striking aspect of the Indian subcontinent, divided since 1947 into two states, India and Pakistan, each of which is still going through the painful process of unification—hampered, in the former, by linguistic differences, and in the latter by geographic division—is the extent to which here East and West have become fused into what one might call an Anglo-Asian synthesis.

When the British, after decades of pressure by the Indian Nationalists, finally relinquished their vast empire and sailed home in August, 1947, ending three centuries of British "presence," it looked as if India would turn its back on its former rulers—as Egypt did when Britain withdrew from the Suez Canal Zone in June 1956—and shut the door on its experience with Britain. Yet, as events proved, nothing could have been further from the truth. The moment the British left, the Indians were free to express their admiration for the practices and institutions Britain had brought to the subcontinent. Today there

[2] From "India and Pakistan: Anglo-Asian Synthesis," chapter 4 from *The Nature of the Non-Western World*, by Vera Micheles Dean, editor of the *Foreign Policy Bulletin*. New American Library (Mentor Book). New York. '57. p 71-82. Reprinted by permission.

is little doubt that India's ideal of democracy is not the United States, but Britain—an ideal which the Indians strive to approach, meanwhile deploring their own shortcomings as judged by British standards.

The basic problem of the Indian subcontinent since the days when Moslem conquerors invaded it from the north in the fifteenth century, establishing the Mogul Empire on the ruins of divided and clashing Hindu principalities, has been the need to reconcile the two principal groups of its vast population, Hindus and Moslems. The differences between these two groups are profound—not only because of differences in their religions, but because their religious and philosophical concepts deeply affect their respective ways of life and their attitudes toward the rest of the world.

When a Westerner first looks at Hinduism and at Islam, the differences seem far more striking and ,far-reaching than the similarities. The Hindus believe in a secular state, and oppose the concept of a state founded on religion. . . . On the other hand, the Moslems of the Indian subcontinent, like their co-religionists elsewhere, think in terms of a religious state. Not only did they insist on the separation of a Moslem state from India, but, once free, they decided that the constitution of Pakistan, with its population of 70 million Moslems and 10 million Hindus, should be squarely based on the Koran, the sacred book of Islam. . . . The religious leaders of Pakistan have gone further than their colleagues of other Moslem states in trying to re-affirm the relations of church and state in the modern world, and in seeking to discover how the precepts of the Koran, through reinterpretation, might be adapted without undue controversy to the recognized needs of the twentieth century. More important, the 40 million Moslems who remained in India are struggling to find a way to preserve their faith and at the same time to achieve political and economic integration with a non-Moslem, predominately Hindu majority.

Hinduism is, in essence, an all-inclusive and all-absorptive religion. It has survived war and civil strife for thousands of years, through countless crises, invasions and conquests, largely because it has proved to be "all things to all men." Within its over-all framework there is room, at one and the same time, in the twentieth century as well as in the distant past, for the beliefs of primitive peoples who worship the forces of nature, believing, like the ancient Greeks, that the Godhead is present in all things, animate and inanimate; yet it also satisfies sophisticated Hindus who want to believe in a supreme being, since it holds that the Godhead is made manifest in human form, notably in the form of Krishna, chief spokesman in the *Bhagavad-Gita.* This brief book, a gem of Hindu literature, is the main part of the *Mahabharata,* one of India's two great epics, the other being the *Ramayana.* . . . The Hindus have always sought to find the common denominator in the many faiths which have flowed into their country from north, east, and west. And even those beliefs which at first appeared to challenge Hinduism on grounds of ideas and practices such as the caste system—notably Buddhism—have ultimately been absorbed into Hinduism and have all but disappeared in India.

By contrast, Islam is a monotheistic faith. When the prophet Mohammed, in the sixth century A.D., interpreted the will of Allah, he thought first of all in terms of purifying Arabic thought of the polytheistic excrescences with which it had become overlaid. It is true that the Koran lists a long roster of prophets drawn from the traditions of other faiths—Christianity and Judaism—including Abraham, Jesus Christ, and the Angel Gabriel, but all these prophets are on a lower level than Allah, the one and only God. And unlike the Hindus, the Moslems do not permit the portrayal of Allah or of his prophet Mohammed.

The devout Hindu is inward-looking. His principal endeavor is to improve himself through pursuit of the path of duty *(dharma)* and the performance of good deeds *(karma)* until such time, with intervening transmigrations of soul, as he can become free of all strife and change, and experience the bliss of *nirvana,* non-being. The Hindu finds nothing peculiar in spending long periods of time in meditation. He is convinced that every deed starts a chain reaction, producing successive resulting situations, and is therefore at great pains to weigh every decision he takes.

At first glance the Moslem seems more akin to the Westerner than the Hindu because of the outward-looking character of his religion. Yet the difference is not as profound as it sometimes appears. In the *Bhagavad-Gita* the god Krishna tells the warrior Arjuna who seeks his counsel on the battlefield that he must act and, if he acts right, he will be reborn. The Moslem, too, is enjoined by the Koran to do good deeds, from giving contributions to religious foundations and alms to the poor to the final and most important act—the journey to Mecca—comparable for the Moslem to the Hindu's pilgrimage to the holy places of his faith, of which the most important is the city of Benares on the Ganges. The Hindus seem to think in abstract terms about good and evil, the retribution of being reborn in an unpleasant form or the rewards of *nirvana*—yet both punishment and reward are vividly anticipated, and practical actions must be taken to achieve the latter rather than the former. Among these is self-training, the use of various disciplines, of which Yoga is one of the best known. The Moslems depict heaven and hell in graphic terms, not unlike those of medieval Christian chronicles. Yet while they represent Allah as a stern taskmaster, the Koran also emphasizes that Allah can be merciful, and that the sinner can obtain mercy by good works. Thus the concepts of life and ethical prescriptions of the two faiths are not, in actuality, as far apart as is sometimes thought in the West.

Hindus seem to differ from Moslems by their emphasis on nonviolence *(ahimsa)* to men and beasts, which is a deeply ingrained principle of Hindu philosophy, as embodied in the Rock Edicts of Hindu Emperor Asoka, and ancient Hindu writings. Because of the injunction not to kill animals, meat eating is prohibited, and respect is enjoined for all animals, but particularly those regarded as sacred—the cow, the snake, and the monkey. The Jains, a reformist Hindu sect, go so far as to forbid deep breathing, for fear that the intake of breath might kill insects invisible to the naked eye. It was this traditional principle of nonviolence which Gandhi invoked when, on his return from South Africa in 1915, he spurred the Congress, organized by the Indian Nationalists, to adopt a policy of nonviolent noncooperation toward the British—a policy which eventually caused the British to withdraw from India.

The Moslems, by contrast, are believed, especially by Hindus, to approve the use of violence. Traditionally, it is true, the followers of Mohammed have supported the idea of waging a holy war—*jihad*—against the infidel. Such a war the Moslems waged against the Christian Crusaders in olden times, and today in Pakistan one can hear talk of *jihad* against India over Kashmir, while Israel fears a holy war against its territory by the Arab states. Yet violence cannot be regarded as an exclusive prerogative of the Moslems. The Hindus, too, have found it difficult to remain nonviolent when their emotions have been deeply stirred. This was seen during the turbulent days of partition in 1947, when the Moslem-Hindu riots shocked and devastated the Indian subcontinent, leaving at the end five or six million homeless, propertyless refugees on both sides of the new border. Again in January 1956 violence characterized the disturbances in Bombay and other leading cities of India, following Nehru's announcement of plans for the reorganization of the country on linguistic lines.

The most striking outward feature which distinguishes Hinduism from Islam in the subcontinent is the existence in India of a caste system, which has never been accepted by the Moslems, either when they lived in India under the British or in the new state of Pakistan. The Moslems believe in the intrinsic equality of man. For them all Moslems, irrespective of rank or wealth or education, are brothers. Only the infidel is an outsider.

In India the caste system, that to Westerners seems peculiar and repugnant, has a significance which is not merely religious, but is also political, economic, and social. It is an institution deeply rooted in the history of the Hindus. Originally the caste system appears to have developed at a time when waves of new immigrants or invaders poured into India. The indigenous people known from the earliest available records must have been small, squat, Negroid in appearance, flat-faced and bushy-haired

—like some of the aborigines who still survive in Australia and the Philippines. Then came the Dravidians (around 3250 B.C.), also dark of skin, but taller and better-formed, who made use of the primitive peoples they found in India in a servile capacity. The Aryans (around 1720 B.C.) who entered from central Asia and were light-skinned and blue-eyed became, in effect, the ruling race, recruiting the natives they found in India to do their less palatable chores and assuming positions of distinctive authority in government, the armed forces, and trade. The result was that Hindu society became divided from top to bottom, according to the lightness or darkness of one's skin, or one's breed: the word *casta,* a Portuguese word, means "breed," while the Hindu word *varna,* used to describe caste, means "color."

The four castes which have persisted into our own times are:

1. *Brahmans* (or Brahmins), who constituted 6 per cent of the population of India before partition, and included in their ranks priests and educators. . . .

2. *Kshatryias,* who are the rulers, nobles, and warriors, form the caste which engaged in civilian and military administration. . . .

3. *Vaishyas,* the caste which includes merchants and landowners, constitutes what we would call in Western societies the middle class.

4. *Sudras,* the workers and servants, were included in the caste system, but had to perform the lowly, hard tasks of Hindu society. . . .

The unique feature of the Indian social system is the fifth group, which was not included in the caste system—the exterior castes also known by the British term "scheduled castes" and the derogatory Hindu phrase "untouchables." Gandhi, shocked by the existence of this sub-proletariat, who were regarded as unclean because they were condemned to perform "unclean" tasks—such as street-sweeping, scavenging, slaughter of animals, tanning, laundry, and so on—called for the abolition of untouchability, and spoke of them as "harijans," children of God.

What made the existence of the untouchables particularly painful was that the Hindu religion, which did not itself prescribe the caste system, nevertheless specified a wide range of prohibitions on contacts between the four castes and the "untouchables," who were confined to jobs regarded as unclean, such as scavenging, on the ground that contacts would bring about pollution of caste members. These prohibitions, in effect, condemned the untouchables to a ghetto existence—to a situation which, in the parlance of modern South African Nationalists, could be described as rigid *apartheid*. The untouchables were forbidden to enter Hindu temples, to use wells, to travel on public conveyances, to live in the same areas of villages and towns as members of other castes, to eat with them, or to intermarry with them, or even to offer them a drink of water. They were excluded from schools, and were even ordered to make a detour on the road if they saw members of castes drawing nigh. True, untouchables, like other Hindus, could achieve a better position through rebirth—but only if they behaved like good untouchables while alive and did not rebel against their lot. Under these circumstances, it is not surprising that some untouchables abandoned Hinduism and turned to other religious faiths.

In their struggle against the concept and practice of the caste system, Gandhi and Nehru won a resounding victory after independence, when the 1950 constitution of the Republic of India prohibited discrimination on grounds of race, religion, or caste. Although this provision has by no means been universally carried out, and many years will elapse before the caste system disappears in India, the system had begun to change even before independence and the adoption of the new constitution.

Many factors caused this process of change, among them the influence of British precept and practice, British insistence on the equality of all individuals before the law, and, above all, the introduction of industrialization, which has gradually whittled down caste restrictions on the use of buses, eating in common, working and living side by side, and other rules which worked a great hardship on untouchables. Moreover, the drift of the untouchables to faiths other than Hinduism—notably Christianity, which did not exclude them from places of wor-

ship, as well as to Islam and, more recently in 1956 to Buddhism
—caused Hindu religious leaders to reconsider their opposition
to the use of temples, and to urge modification of ancient rules.
And the Indian government's insistence on equal educational
opportunities for all is gradually breaking down the barriers, in
schools and colleges, that once made it well-nigh impossible for
untouchables to obtain the education without which they could
not hope to gain the skills that, in turn, would make it possible
for them to rise in the economic and social scale.

Thus, India is passing through a profound social revolution, which may ultimately bring about the breakdown of the
caste system. This revolution should not be too rapid and
violent according to responsible Indians, who point out that
with all its reprehensible features, the caste system has served
to hold together widely diverse populations, has provided a
cement for a society which might otherwise disintegrate, and
has acted as a voluntary social security system, with each member
of a caste feeling responsibility for the poor or handicapped
among his fellow caste members. Only when India has succeeded in providing substitutes for the advantages offered by
the caste—such as its social security aspect—would it be wise,
they feel, to discard the system. Moreover, some observers
believe that, as India becomes industrialized, its population may
divide along class, instead of caste, lines, and that then the
newly emerging classes may clash with each other, as has happened in more advanced countries at comparable stages of
economic and social development.

The two philosophies of Hinduism and Islam are reflected
in the nature of the two new states—India and Pakistan—
which emerged after the withdrawal of Britain in 1947. The
Republic of India was established by a constitution proclaimed
three years after partition. This constitution is squarely based
on the principles of political democracy as developed in India
under British rule, and enlarged by the Indians to include the
concepts of economic and social democracy. . . . The Indian
constitution combines Gandhi's ideas about nonviolence and the
protection of minority groups, notably the untouchables; Nehru's

belief in a moderate form of socialism, deeply influenced by the ideas and practices of the British Laborites; and some of the basic principles of British administration, particularly the rule of law. It thus represents a synthesis of the most advanced thinking of Britain and Asia.

WHY INDIA WAS PARTITIONED [3]

The background of Hindu-Moslem separation goes back nearly a thousand years. . . . Numberless examples of fast friendship between Hindus and Moslems can be found, but the fact remains that the two communities, broadly speaking, never got along. . . .

Bloody clashes between adherents of the two faiths have marred the Indian scene for many generations. These sanguinary riots have often been religious in origin, as when Moslems slaughtered cows, which the Hindus hold sacred, or cut limbs from a holy *peepul* tree so that a procession might pass; or when Hindus, celebrating one of their festivals, made a racket outside a mosque during the prayer hour.

Hope that Hindus and Moslems might find a way of living together was doomed in 1937, when governments formed by the National Congress, which included Moslems as well as Hindus, shut out the Moslems in some of the newly autonomous provinces. At this time Mohammed Ali Jinnah, formerly a Congress leader, and his Moslem League became implacably committed to Pakistan.

Convinced that Moslems would never get a square deal in a predominantly Hindu India, Jinnah pressed the "two-nation theory" as a basis for partition. Eventually, when there seemed to be no other way to end British rule on the subcontinent, Congress agreed to the creation of a Pakistan to be made up of predominantly Moslem provinces and such doubtful areas as might choose to join the new Islamic state through a plebiscite. But the Congress, and Nehru in particular, never accepted the

[3] From *India Since Independence,* pamphlet by Robert Trumbull, correspondent of the New York *Times.* (Headline Series) Foreign Policy Association. New York. My.-Je. '54. p 4-10. Reprinted by permission.

two-nation theory. This is the basis of India's claim to the predominantly Moslem state of Kashmir today. . . .

Continued condemnation of the two-nation theory by Nehru and millions of other Hindus has caused many Pakistanis to fear that India still hopes some day to annex Pakistan and restore the historic borders of the former British realm. Meanwhile, fanatic utterances of extremists in Pakistan have inevitably brought accusations from the Hindus in India that the Moslems hope to see the crescent of Islam fly again over the symbolic Red Fort of the Mogul emperors in Delhi.

When partition did take place in 1947 it was not possible to delimit territory so that all the Moslems would be on one side, all Hindus on the other. The final determination of boundaries by a commission with a British chairman—the decisions were invariably his, since the Hindu and Moslem members could never agree on anything—left both sides dissatisfied. . . .

The job of apportioning all the assets of government, down to pencils and filing cabinets, was an appalling one and has never been properly finished. Even prisoners and lunatics were exchanged by the two new governments.

The Jinnah regime labored under the immense disadvantage of having to set up an administration from scratch in Karachi, Pakistan's capital, lacking even desks and chairs for high-level civil officers. New Delhi was already a going concern, with all facilities set in place. By contrast, Pakistan had to construct virtually overnight the entire framework of government for the world's seventh largest nation.

Many riots had preceded partition, as the agitation for Pakistan grew. With Moslem demands satisfied, the disturbances abated. But when partition was accomplished, blood began to flow again in the Punjab.

Partition Riots

In the Punjab, Moslem attacks on the Sikhs were at the bottom of the clashes that led to carnage. The Sikh sect, a reformed off-shoot of Hinduism, was founded in the fifteenth century. Most of its six million adherents live in the Punjab, forming a prosperous, homogeneous and powerful community. The partition line cut across Sikh lands, leaving the richest farms in Moslem Pakistan. This automatically divided the Sikh population between two sovereign states, with a consequent weakening of its political solidarity. Sikh antagonism to Moslems dated back to persecution of the sect by the seventeenth-century Mogul emperor, Aurangzeb. Besides, it was the powerful Sikh kingdom, extending over almost the whole of present Western Pakistan, which was one of the last to fall to the British (1849) in the period of the consolidation of their power in India.

Whether the Sikhs on the Indian side of the border drove out the hated Moslems, or envious and greedy Moslems attacked the wealthier Sikhs in Pakistan, is now an academic question. The Punjab burst into flames, and the conflagration immediately engulfed the North. Blood ran in Delhi and the United Provinces, and reached to Pakistan's North-West Frontier Province. Every kind of horror was enacted on both sides, and no member of the minority community breathed easily. A terrified exodus began by every kind of conveyance and afoot. Families piled their movable possessions into bullock carts, forming miserable caravans, sixty miles or more long, choking the Punjab roads and moving in both directions. Railway trains were attacked in the desert, and in cities station platforms were often red with blood.

Millions of people on both sides lost everything they possessed except what they could carry in their flight—with what bitterness one may imagine. . . . The heartbreak, visible as these displaced persons inquire about old friends and places dear to them that they will probably never see again, is pitiful. Many of them have commented about the greater tragedy of their children growing up as strangers to their ancestral land, even learning to hate people and places that their parents loved. The reservoir of affection that remains between Pakistan and India through ancient personal ties is sadly ebbing with the current generation.

Problems of Partition

The enormous forced exchange of populations, 6 million Moslems from India to Pakistan, 5 million Hindus and Sikhs from Pakistan to India, confronted the two new governments with problems which neither anticipated and for which they were unprepared. . . . Economic problems that the refugees brought in their train demanded heroic efforts of governments that would have been sorely tried even by the normal exigencies of the times, to which were added the burdens of partition and the formation of a new state. Few people abroad realize how bravely India and Pakistan coped with this emergency. . . .

Today there are practically no Sikhs, and few Hindus, to be found in West Pakistan. In East Bengal, the eastern wing of Pakistan, about ten million Hindus remain. New rioting broke out in East Bengal and Calcutta in the winter of 1949-1950 but was ended with the "Charter for Minorities" drawn up by Nehru and the late Prime Minister Liaquat Ali Khan of Pakistan in New Delhi in April 1950. However, the state of mind among the rival religious communities gives little cause for satisfaction. Disturbances on a small scale still break out here and there. Although quickly put down, they leave one conscious of ancient fires smoldering underneath.

Even without the obvious economic difficulties inherent in partition, to say nothing of the unforeseen catastrophe of the riots and migrations, the formula evolved for freeing the sub-continent of British rule was an awkward one. The two parts of Pakistan are separated by a thousand miles of Indian territory, with no land corridor between. East Pakistan, in turn, cuts off all but a narrow sliver of Assam from the rest of India. This has caused great disruption of India's economy in that area.

The partition had drastic economic effects on the two new nations. Broadly speaking, Pakistan got the better cotton-, food- and jute-producing area; India, the coal, metals and industrial resources of the subcontinent. The old pattern was also shattered in the military sense. India retained the principal reservoir of fighting manpower as well as the industries that would support a defense effort, but the traditional invasion routes, notably the famous Khyber Pass, are in Pakistani territory. While common sense might suggest complementary economic and defense arrangements, it was not long before the two countries had broken off trade and their armies were fighting each other in Kashmir.

Armed hostilities were halted by the intercession of the United Nations Security Council. But commerce, although restored to a large extent, has been diverted from the normal easy channels by the desire of both countries to become self-sufficient and to find alternative markets which would reduce their natural inter-dependence.

GANDHI'S INFLUENCE [4]

[Immediately after India gained independence, Gandhi, the father of his country, was assassinated by a fanatical Hindu nationalist.—Ed.]

Mahatma Gandhi was not only the hero and saint of modern India but, you might say, of the whole of modern Asia. . . . This position not only as father of his own country but as a sort of inspirer for the whole of Asia was a result of almost eighty years of life which had been devoted to freedom for the people of India—freedom through right and justice and with certain ethical basis. In fact, it was always very difficult to make out whether Mahatma Gandhi was a religious phenomenon, a social reformer, or a politician. From my own point of view, and I only saw him at the very end of his life, he was not a politician at all. But it may be that this complete absence of politics or not thinking of politics may have been the most consummate form of politics—I don't know.

At all events, by seeming to consider only ethical matters, the good, the true, and the beautiful, and what was right, by these means, this saint and hero achieved an unrivaled power over the masses of the people. So that he had only to express a very mild opinion in a very mild manner to get the whole of the 400 million people of India to do what he wanted. This is the kind of thing that happened over and over again and provided the unique basis of his great influence. Gandhi never held a public office. He was never elected to anything or appointed to anything and he only once went into the parliament of India, during the days when they already had a parliament under the British rule. He went as a guest, as a tourist, mainly to see

[4] From "Assignment . . . Nehru," interview, August 21, 1959, by Vincent Sheean, author and foreign correspondent. Westinghouse Broadcasting Company. 122 E. 42d St. New York 17. '59. p 1-6. Reprinted by permission.

what it was like. Otherwise, he knew nothing of such things and never took part in any political elections. His influence on other matters, on the social life and ethics of the people was tremendous.

He began, of course, with nonviolence. That was his main contribution to the idea of the struggle for freedom. He trained his own followers and through them increased numbers of thousands of others to a method of nonviolent passive resistance or voluntary sacrifice, whatever you want to call it, which is unique in history; so that hundreds of thousands of people actually would go out into the streets in front of the British policemen and violate some simple law such as the law against the making of salt. They would go out and make salt in the street and get arrested for it and go to jail until every jail in India was full and it was impossible to go on any longer. This was the technique of nonviolence which used to be called by our own Thoreau in America "passive resistance." It has been called different things in different countries but never has it achieved such a historical effectiveness, such an activity in depth and width as it did in India during the thirty years of the national revolution. Gandhi led this revolution, sometimes without seeming to do so. Even from retirement and by means of prayer and meditation, he was actually directing the national movement for the freedom of India. He, of course, went to prison many times, but so did . . . the present Prime Minister Jawaharlal Nehru, . . . the closest follower of Mahatma Gandhi. I say the closest in the sense that he has, in most people's eyes, become the successor to Mahatma Gandhi as the leader of the Indian people. Now a line must be drawn, of course. Mr. Nehru is an extremely practical man and he is a politician as Mahatma was not. Mr. Nehru has been in politics all his life and his father was before him. He was born in politics the way the fish is born in the sea. The difference, of course, is great. And yet we must all remember that Mahatma Gandhi said many times over "Jawaharlal is my heir"; at other times, he said, "Jawaharlal is my political heir," thus seeming to make a difference between the social and religious aspect of his teaching

and the straight political. Whether we put in the word political
or whether we leave it out, it is obvious that in the Mahatma's
eyes, Jawaharlal was his heir.

The years since Gandhi's death have been more or less the
years (almost exactly the years) in which India has gradually
assumed its present position, and its present significance in
the world. Jawaharlal Nehru more than any other one person
has come to represent India to the world and to India itself,
it's fair to say; because even Mr. Gandhi never had a more
direct power of influence on the Indian mind in the depart-
ments which Nehru is concerned with than Nehru does. Nobody in India today can call forth the tremendous enthusiasm
that he evokes among the people wherever he goes or when-
ever he speaks to them. . . .

Now there are many questions we have to ask Mr. Nehru. . . .

SHEEAN: Well, Prime Minister, I want to begin by asking
you if the government of India is still dominated by the ideas
of Mahatma Gandhi?

NEHRU: That is rather a difficult question to answer. I
would say that India as a whole is dominated by the personality
of Gandhi still and is powerfully influenced by many of his basic
ideas and in that sense the government of India is also influenced
by the memory of his personality and some basic ideas. But
I don't think it would be correct to say that all we do are in
consequence of Gandhi's ideas, because conditions change and
we have naturally to consider matters in their present context.
I don't know what Gandhi might have said in regard to any
particular matter now but the basic ideas of his would no
doubt have remained. Also, it is rather difficult for any government to function on the level of a saint.

SHEEAN: About nonviolence. For example, many of us
who had deep reverence for the Mahatma have wondered if
it would suit all situations. Do you think that it does win,
that it is bound to win in the end?

NEHRU: Well, in theory, yes. But in practice so much depends upon the people who do it—their training, their powers
of resistance without becoming afraid and running away or

retaliating. You will remember that Gandhi said that "Non-violence is not a coward's remedy. It is a brave man's remedy," and if you have cowardice or fear in your heart, it is better to be violent than to pretend to be nonviolent. So it depends really on the people, and it requires, I suppose, a great deal of training for the people to function on that high level.

SHEEAN: Years of effort.

NEHRU: Yes, and character and all that. Not only years of effort but, well, certain basic characteristics which they may or may not have.

SHEEAN: On the side of disarmament which I have heard often discussed, I have heard you rule that out. Does armament or disarmament seem to you to involve the Gandhian ideas, or having an army and navy conflict with those ideas?

NEHRU: I have no doubt whatever that Gandhi would have been all in favor of one-sided disarmament, being sure that this itself would produce a reaction on the other side. He would do the right thing and face the consequences with faith. But it is a kind of thing that governments normally cannot do. They have to deal with people's reactions. And I am not aware of any government that dares to do it. The most that you can say is that a government should be constantly thinking of this problem and wanting to do so with the best of its ability.

INDIA'S LEADER—NEHRU [5]

The Prime Minister of India has spent much of his lifetime studying what makes Jawaharlal Nehru tick and so far this expert has come up with no better analysis than the common one that he is a very complex individual, "a blend of East and West at home nowhere." Speaking of himself a few weeks ago, Nehru remarked that he was "no true representative of India." He added: "I realize that and I always try to understand it, try to accept it, try to imbibe it. To some extent I succeed. . . ."

[5] From "An Enigma Caught in a Dilemma," by Robert Trumbull, correspondent. New York *Times Magazine.* p 11+. O. 4, '59. Reprinted by permission.

Two individuals, it is said, have had the most influence in shaping Nehru's political beliefs. The first was George Bernard Shaw, who led him through an early radical period. The second was Mohandas Gandhi, who taught him that wrong means are never justified by right ends.

What remains of the first phase in Nehru's development would no doubt enable him to be a Communist today. But what remains of the second makes this impossible.

So one finds Nehru, in his seventieth year, displaying an unusual tolerance of communism and freely admitting that he still finds certain of its social theories attractive (though by now he has created his own interpretation of these theories, which differs from those of Khrushchev and Mao).

On the other hand, Nehru reveals a strong abhorrence of communism's methods. He all but strong-arms the Communist party of his own country (from 1949 to 1951, there were more Communists in jail in India than in any other country except possibly the Soviet Union), but he bristles ferociously at any attempt to draw him into common cause with the Western free nations against the international Communist movement directed from Moscow and Peiping.

These are questions concerning Nehru's cerebral processes to be returned to later. To understand him in world politics, it is first necessary to consider the man in the light of his place in his own country.

To the outside world, Nehru is "Mister India." But apart from his relationship with a certain restricted circle of Indians, he is temperamentally—and in other ways—as alien to his surroundings as the American correspondents who travel with him; in some respects, more so. . . .

With little more to go on than certain universally shared political aspirations and the uniting influence of a more or less common cultural background, Nehru has come a long way, since India gained independence in 1947, in welding the brawling mass into a unified republic. His task is far from done. One wonders who, after Nehru, could override the sectional cleavages of India by force of personality, as he has done.

The unparalleled scope of Nehru's personal acquaintanceship with every part of India, coupled with his perceptive grasp of history here and elsewhere, must be numbered among the elements that govern his approach to world affairs. But there are other factors that make it difficult to see how his personality could be expected to fit into any but its own unique mold.

Nehru's sensitive mind, it must be remembered, dwells in a vessel that is the product of centuries of breeding. As a Kashmiri Brahman he is an aristocrat of aristocrats who could hardly have grown to manhood without a share of the arrogance and pride that go with the consciousness of superior birth and upbringing. He would be an even rarer type of individual than he is if this weren't so.

Brought up in a wealthy household with English governesses, Nehru's mind was nurtured in the most Westernized of Indian circles. His father, Motilal Nehru, was a brilliant lawyer who was said to have shared bottles of champagne with his British jailers when he was a political prisoner.

When young Jawaharlal went off to school in England the boy moved naturally into high social and intellectual circles. His father, a contemporary has recalled, asked friends in London to keep an eye on him and was delighted to hear that his son had learned to appreciate fine wine. Today, as head of a government with a policy of prohibition (adopted against the Prime Minister's personal inclination, it is said), Nehru isn't seen with a glass in his hand containing anything stronger than fruit juice.

The following years, as has been noted, whirled young Nehru into the fashionable circle of Fabian socialism, from which he has never entirely departed intellectually. On his return to India, he was drawn naturally into the independence movement. There he came under the eye of Gandhi, who pushed him to the top in Indian politics, even though Nehru often disagreed violently with his mentor on matters of policy, generally in local contexts.

During the early part of this period in his political career Nehru saw the world—the Western part of it, at any rate—as sliding toward a division between fascism and communism. His outlook went through a series of interesting shadings in an evolution that is still going on.

In 1923, addressing a Congress party meeting, Nehru declared that "bolshevism and fascism . . . are really alike and represent different phases of insensate violence and intolerance." This was a phase in his thinking that soon gave way to a new appraisal expressed in a statement ten years later: "I do believe that fundamentally the choice before the world today is between some form of communism and some form of fascism and I am all for the former, i.e., communism." But a quarter of a century later he was far closer to his 1923 estimate.

Meanwhile he had made his first visit to Soviet Russia. His adherence to the Communist aspiration toward a classless society—an ideal he still holds—didn't blind him to the excesses of the Soviet regime. These have evoked a progressive repulsion in Nehru to the present day.

He also recoils sharply from the doctrinaire aspect of Communist teachings and the intellectual regimentation inherent in the party practice. He was saying as much twenty years ago and he is saying it more forcefully now. "Marx," he has declared repeatedly in recent years, "is out of date." He has accused the Communists in India of being the "real reactionaries" in holding to economic theories that no longer apply to conditions existing today. . . .

If Nehru feels this way about communism why doesn't he bring India in on the side of the West in the cold war? The answer can be summed up in a few words. In the first place, he is convinced that the cold war is the worst thing that the world faces today, because in his view any problem brought into the purview of the East-West conflict immediately becomes insoluble, even if it was not before. Secondly, he does not think that communism, in its present phase of violence and contention, is going to last.

"In spite of the rigidity of the Communist party and its creed," he said to India's Parliament a few weeks ago, "I think,

and history teaches us also, that all this so-called rigidity becomes flexible by the force of events. . . . So I do not believe
that anything is rigid for long in the changing world. And
therefore I have always expected and hoped for a progressive
reasonableness, even in the rigid Communist approach.". . .

Nehru has both a philosophical and a practical attachment
to coexistence. To take up the practical first, he is aware that
if the ultimate alternative to coexistence should be war, then
the beginning of the fighting would mark the end of India's
desperate struggle to raise the level of living of her peoples.
And this in turn might well spell the doom of the Indian
Republic as it exists today. This is the more obvious basis for
Nehru's policy of nonalignment, often miscalled "neutralism."

But this policy has deeper roots. It has been hardened by
long personal observation of his country's built-in elements of
clash.

There is no hope for India except in terms of coexistence between
different provinces, different groups, different languages, different habits
. . . [he declared recently] but . . . there has been that philosophical
approach to coexistence in India for long ages past. In spite of India
being split up into many states, many kingdoms . . . it is a certain
approach to coexistence and toleration that has carried on through. . . .

How does Nehru really stand on cold war issues now that
he himself is a target of the Soviet Union's Asian partner?
Probably as he always has, it seems to this observer. His sym-
pathies basically lie with the West, whose political forms are
those of Nehru's India, although he may take sharp issue with
Washington and London on specific questions and will refuse
to commit himself to any alliance that confines him. But on
Nehru's political philosophy one may well quote Ellsworth
Bunker, the United States Ambassador in New Delhi: "No
one is more dedicated to the process of democracy than Nehru."

INDIA'S CONSTITUTION [6]

The fifteenth of August, 1947, is one of the most significant
dates in history, for it was on that date that India, under the

[6] From "Constitution, Government and Democratic Ideals of India," by P. N.
Sapru, member of Indian Parliament. New York Times. Sec. 10. p 13+. Ja. 25,
'59.

arrangement embodied with the mutual consent of Indian leaders and the British government, in the Independence Act of 1947, became completely free to determine her destiny.

The silent revolution which the founding fathers brought about in the governance of this country with the goodwill and assent of the British government and people was not what would be called a Marxist-Leninist revolution. The founding fathers had derived principally their inspiration in their days of struggle from democratic thinkers and writers.

It was inevitable, therefore, that the constitution when framed should have provided this country with a sovereign democratic republic pledged to promote justice, social, political and economic, and uphold the dignity of the individual and the unity of the nation. It is vital to note that according to the Indian theory the constitution as finally framed proceeded from the Indian people.

Quasi-federal Constitution

A casual glance at the constitution will show that it is a quasi-federal one, for it normally provides for a division of sovereignty between the Union Center and its various units—that is to say, its states.

The President

The executive authority of the Union has been vested in the president whose position will roughly correspond to that of the French president or the British king. The president has to be elected by the lower houses of the various states, as also the two houses of parliament. He has a vice president elected by the two houses of the Union legislature to assist him.

The constitution enjoins the president to select as his prime minister the person who is in a position to command a majority in the House of the People. The prime minister chooses his colleagues and they are collectively responsible to the Lok Sabha —i.e., the House of the People.

Parliament

There is at the Union Center a bicameral system. The House of the People has a membership of 500 elected on the basis of universal suffrage by territorial constituencies. The Council of States, which represents the states of the Indian Union, is for the most part indirectly elected on the basis of proportional representation by state legislatures. It has a few nominated members to represent science, art, literature and social service. In order to become an act, a bill has to be assented to by both the houses.

Special Features

Two special features of the constitution which deserve attention are the provisions in regard to (a) fundamental rights and (b) the directive principles of state policy. The Indian constitution not merely enunciates these rights but it has also given a right to persons affected by their infringement to go to the higher courts of the land for their enforcement. The fundamental rights conceded by the constitution include the right of freedom of speech and expression; of assembling peaceably and without arms; of forming associations or unions; of moving freely throughout the territory of India; of acquiring, holding and disposing of property; and of practicing any profession, or of carrying on any occupation, trade or business. The constitution provides both for equality before the law and the equal protection of the laws.

The constitution lays down that reasonable restrictions can be placed upon these rights in the interests of public order or morality, and it is for the higher courts, at the apex of which is the Supreme Court, to determine in a case coming up before them whether the restriction is reasonable or not. In this respect there is much similarity between our constitution and that of the United States, and often in the arguments, as also in the judgments of our courts references are made to decisions of the U.S. Supreme Court and other state supreme courts. Owing to this power of judicial review the judiciary has come to occupy an important place in our constitution. An important point which needs to be emphasized is that untouchability, which has been a blot on Indian civilization, has been declared illegal by the constitution, and that strict efforts are made by courts and other authorities to see that this directive is carried out.

Civil Services

For the carrying on of the administration of the country India has regularly formed civil services. The running of a department or the administration of a district is a great co-operative enterprise in which both the ministers and the officials share. For the selection of the services, there are public service commissions both at the Center and in the states which have been made independent by the constitution of the control of the executive power.

System of Audit

The constitution also provides for an independent system of audit under the supervision of the auditor general. His status and position have been laid down by the constitution itself. A new innovation is the appointment of a linguistic minorities commissioner who has to report to the president regarding the position of the various regional languages in this country.

Secular Character

A word must be said about the secular character of the Indian republic. In the Indian subcontinent we have several religions. All of them have been given a place of equality. There can be no discrimination against any person on the ground of his religion or caste. The state pursues a policy of strict neutrality or impartiality towards all religions. Religious minorities are entitled to have denominational schools or institutions of their own and to propagate their religion in such a manner as not to endanger public safety. In villages an attempt has been made to revive civic life by the institution of elected panchayats [village councils] with limited judicial powers.

Spirit of Democracy

Clearly the Indian constitution is permeated with the spirit of democracy and liberalism. Its philosophy is based upon the view that liberty and equality are both equally important. In a country which was left by the accidents of history behind in the struggle for existence, it has become important to plan objectives for higher standards of living. With the success on the economic front of these plans is bound up the future of democracy in India.

PARTIES AND POLITICS IN INDIA [7]

Indian political life appears to the outsider as something tame, dominated by a single party, the Congress, which in itself is generally believed to be the instrument of Pandit Jawaharlal Nehru. This is, in fact, a grave misconception. Because it is a federal union, the outside public thinks of India only in terms of federal policies, foreign affairs, economic planning and is generally unaware of the fact that the active area of politics lies in the states whose governments are directly in touch with the people and whose activities touch their daily lives.

The states of India that constitute the Union are, many of them, larger than the great states of Europe. For example, Uttar Pradesh has a population of 65 million, Bihar and Bombay each have over 50 million while the smallest state in area, Kerala, has a population of 14 million. It is obvious that to look upon or judge the politics of India from the angle of the Central Government would be unreal and distorted.

The existence of a great national party (the Congress), in power in all but one of the sixteen states, and its continued and effective leadership by Mr. Nehru, have so far obscured this significant fact. But although the National Congress is a well-integrated institution which lays down and coordinates national policies, it is necessary to remember that its organization is based primarily on the states and it is the work of the party in the states that gives it strength and prestige.

[7] From article by K. M. Panikkar, former Indian ambassador to France. *Current History*. 36:153-7. Mr. '59. Reprinted by permission.

Nor is it wholly correct to hold that Mr. Nehru's power is absolute over the Congress. The immense prestige he enjoys in the country and the affection and confidence which the Indian people, without reference to parties and politics, show to him have today given him an authority, which no one except Mahatma Gandhi ever enjoyed. This does not arise from his leadership of the Congress. The fact that he grew up with the national movement and was one of its effective leaders in the struggle for independence has naturally made the common man in India identify him with achievements of independence itself. . . .

Though his leadership of the Congress is not seriously challenged today, it is an error to conclude that his authority in the party is absolute. Apart from his own firm attachment to democratic principles and his consequent refusal to force his own views on the party, there have been numerous instances during the last five years when Nehru has had to compromise with opposition in his own party. Two outstanding instances will suffice to prove this point. During the period of public discussion relating to the reorganization of the states of India Mr. Nehru strongly advocated a policy of creating bigger units by the amalgamation of Bengal and Bihar in the east and Madras and Kerala in the south. But the opposition within the Congress proved to be too powerful and the project was quietly abandoned. Again, when it was known that the President, Dr. Rajendra Prasad, was not desirous of being reelected Mr. Nehru strongly recommended Dr. Radhakrishnan, the Vice President, as the head of the state. But in view of the feeling inside the party that Dr. Rajendra Prasad should continue as President, Mr. Nehru withdrew his original proposal and accepted the view of the party.

Mr. Nehru is no authoritarian leader. The high command of the Congress, even after eleven years of independence, contains many leaders who were Mr. Nehru's colleagues in the freedom struggle, who enjoy great prestige in the country and whose influence in the determination of policies is considerable. The federal character of the state which encourages the growth

of provincial leadership is also a major factor to be considered
in estimating Nehru's effective power in the country.

When all this is said, Mr. Nehru remains a leader of unique
authority in India, enjoying the confidence of the people as a
whole. Every major aspect of India's national activities during
the last twelve years is identified with him: planned economic
development, large-scale industrialization, the development of
scientific research, progress in atomic work, the great social revolution inaugurated by the reform of Hindu law and the trans-
formation of the village through community projects. All this
has been inspired by him and identified with his personal leadership by the country as a whole.

A further significant fact about Nehru is that though he
is the unchallenged leader of a party, he also enjoys the position
of being a national arbiter. While other parties in the country
freely criticize the policies of his government, all parties, including the Communists, look to him to ensure that the scale is
not weighted against them. . . .

No one who steps into Mr. Nehru's place as prime minister
can expect to succeed to this unique position; and that is why
the question, "who after Nehru?" is often raised, more outside
India than within the country. . . .

The answer seems to be clear. Democracy is essentially a
political system of dispersed leadership. The unique leader,
who symbolizes and represents the nation, is important only in
a period of national crisis. At the start of India's independence,
when her territory was being integrated, her democratic institutions developing and the major lines of development in the
economic and social spheres shaping up—apart, of course, from
the numerous problems arising from the partition—it was essential that the conutry should be guided by a leader of exceptional prestige, enjoying unchallenged authority. But the success of democratic processes depends not on exceptional leaders,
but on the availability of leadership at all levels. The questions that India has to face in this connection are two: Does the
experience of the last eleven years show that Indian democracy
provides opportunities for the development of this type of

leadership and, secondly, does the Indian political system provide for the automatic selection of such a leader when the time comes?

New Leadership

It is foolish to be dogmatic about the future, but today a clear answer to both these questions is possible. The last few years have witnessed the emergence of new and younger leaders, capable of guiding India along democratic lines. It is necessary to emphasize once again the federal character of the Indian structure—a situation similar to that of the United States. It is not to the federal parliament, or to the central government of India that we should look for the leaders of the future. It is in the constituent states of the federation that new leadership manifests itself.

The Center itself recruits its more important ministers from among those who have shown notable political and administrative capacity in state governments. . . . The problem, therefore, is whether the state governments have been throwing up new men who can in time take the place of the leaders who came to the forefront during the period of India's national struggle. The question can, I think, only be answered in the affirmative, when it is realized that in such important states as Bombay, Madras, Andhra, Mysore, Kerala and Rajasthan the leadership is in the hands of men who have achieved political prominence after independence.

The second question is, does India have the machinery for selecting leaders when the time comes? The political parties in India are well enough organized to make a selection on a democratic basis for the acceptance of parliament, and the danger, therefore, of any kind of interregnum or the failure of leadership can be discounted. At all times the Congress and, following the Congress, the other political parties, have had a democratic and collective leadership. Even under Mahatma Gandhi this was an outstanding fact in India's political life. "Who after Nehru?" is, therefore, a question, which while undoubtedly important, does not seem to involve any danger to India's democratic development or her political stability. . . .

The Congress Party

The dominant position of the Indian National Congress among the political parties in India developed primarily from its historic role in the struggle for national independence. Founded in 1885, it has reflected every stage in the growth of India's modern nationhood. After 1920, when Mahatma Gandhi took over its effective leadership, converted it into a mass organization and made it an instrument for the achievement of independence, the Congress became identified with the nation. But it should not be forgotten that until the eve of independence the Congress was not a party in the ordinary sense. It was a national movement which reflected practically every shade of opinion: from the extreme conservatives to the Socialists, the Communists having been excluded only during the war when they decided on a policy of cooperation with the British.

It was one of Mr. Nehru's achievements to have gradually converted this national movement into a political party with a definite program covering all aspects of national life. The prestige of the Congress and the personality of Pandit Nehru have enabled it, even after its conversion to a political party, to maintain its hold on public imagination.

There are two aspects of the organization of the Congress which should be emphasized. The first is its democratic character. It is organized horizontally with district, provincial and All India Congress Committees, all elected on a nominal franchise—reflecting in effect the federal character of the Indian government. Secondly, its top leadership has always been collective. Not only are questions discussed openly in the All India Congress Committee which meets at regular intervals, but the President of the Congress is assisted by a working committee which consists of the main personalities of the party and has a broad territorial representation. These two features enable the party to reconcile national leadership with territorial interests.

Is the Congress hold on the country weakening? Before a definite conclusion can be reached on this important question it is necessary to consider the following factors. In transform-

ing the Congress from a movement into a party, its leaders not
only foresaw but may be said to have encouraged the creation
of other parties with alternative programs appealing for support to the country. Secondly, the Congress, in power for over
eleven years, has suffered like every other political party from a
reaction in the country. Thirdly, as a democratic organization,
it is given to a great deal of self-criticism.

No one does this more effectively or more often than Mr.
Nehru himself who is continuously pointing out to his followers
the weaknesses, the loss of dynamism, the struggle for power
inside the party, the failure to maintain contact with the masses
and other obvious shortcomings of a party long in power. But
it should not be forgotten that these criticisms are meant to
awaken the party to its sense of responsibility, and must be
considered mainly as self-criticism. Though the Congress has
lost some of its prestige in the states as a result of local conditions, broadly speaking it would be a mistake to consider that its
hold on the country as a whole has weakened to any considerable
degree.

Opposition Parties

Two other parties claim our attention because they challenge
the authority of the Congress; the P.S.P. (or the Praja Socialist
Party) and the Communists. Both these parties are organized
nationally. Except for the Communists in Kerala, they have
made no serious dent on the authority of the Congress; yet they
polled a significant percentage of the votes cast in the general
election. The P.S.P. which is a splinter party of the Congress
suffers from the fact that there is no major difference in policy
between it and the parent organization.

The Communist Party

The Communist party of India deserves much greater consideration. Its activities started seriously in the 1930's, but it
had no national policy beyond that of carrying out the orders of
the Third International, received through British intermediaries.
Its attempt to penetrate the Congress did not meet with any great

success, and consequently it did not count in national politics.
But the war provided it with an opportunity. As long as Russia
remained out of it, the Communists denounced the war as imperialist but after Hitler's attack on the Soviet Union, they became enthusiastic supporters of the war effort and worked in
close cooperation with the British authorities in India. As a
result of this strange and unnatural alliance against the national
movement, the Communist party emerged after the war greatly
discredited.

Nor were its actions in the period immediately following independence of a kind to win national favor. During the first
three years of independence, the party followed a policy of
"adventurism," of violence, industrial sabotage, wrecking of railways, and so on, with the object of creating chaos in the country,
because the Communists proclaimed that the independence India
had achieved had not liberated the people but had tied them
more closely to British capitalism. But a change in tactics came
with the promulgation of the new constitution. The party decided to contest the elections and though the Congress victory
was overwhelming, in a few areas the Communists were able
to gain some notable successes.

In the second general election in the spring of 1957, the
party was able to gain a notable success in Kerala; with the
help of a few independents the Communists took over the administration. The experiment of a Communist government
operating within the framework of a democratic parliamentary
system, facing a vigilant opposition and with an independent
judiciary deciding on the legality of the government's actions is,
indeed, unique. [The Communist government in Kerala has since
been displaced. See "Communism in India," in Section II, below.—Ed.]

Both the P.S.P. and the Communists are important factors
in India's national life, providing not only an effective opposition, but ensuring a progressive attitude on the part of the
Congress in respect to the economic and social development
of the country. It is likely that in the next election they may

strengthen their position in some of the provinces. . . . But the prospect of their assuming power in the majority of states or in the Central Government seems to be negligible.

Provincial Groups

Outside these three All India parties there are also certain provincial organizations which are not without significance in local politics. The Jan Sangh or people's party is, broadly speaking, a conservative organization, which speaks for orthodox Hindus. Its influence is mainly around Delhi, and its strength is derived from the large number of displaced persons from West Punjab (Pakistan), concentrated in that area. In the province of Orissa a new party (organized mainly by the dispossessed princes who controlled the major part of that area before India's independence) forms the main opposition to the Congress, and though its political significance is not very great the chances of its displacing the Congress in the area should not be overlooked.

Non-communal Politics

Finally, one very important aspect of political life in India after her independence remains to be emphasized. During the period of British rule, political parties, apart from the Congress, were organized on a communal basis to represent the interests of the different communities in India. Hindus, Moslems, Christians, Sikhs and Scheduled Castes (untouchables) had their separate organizations which tended to emphasize the divisive tendencies in the country rather than national feeling. With independence and the development of a secular political life, the separate organization of communities has practically vanished. The Hindu Mahasabha continued for a time, until it was wiped out in the general elections. The Moslem League lost its purpose with the creation of Pakistan, and today exists only in name in Madras and Kerala. The case of the Scheduled Castes (untouchables) and Christian organizations is similar, and though some Sikh leaders continue to claim special privileges, the importance of their organization has greatly diminished with the growth of non-communal secular politics.

Briefly, although Nehru's personality and his prestige in the country help to overshadow other parties, the growth of political life in India and the strength of democratic forces working at all levels from the village to the national government have contributed to the growth of a healthy party system. While the party system so far has not been particularly effective at the center, it has functioned with notable results in the states. It is unlikely that in the near future the Congress will be displaced as the leading party organization, even after Mr. Nehru's leadership ends. The growth of these All India parties, generally to the Left of the Congress, has prevented the Congress from losing touch with the people and from becoming an oligarchy.

INDIA'S EXPLODING POPULATION [8]

Human fertility is a potent force which will control India's destiny during the next thirty years.

Should her high birth rate remain at its present level and her death rate continue to decline, India's population will almost double by 1986. Nearly 800 million people will live in an area about two fifths the size of the United States.

Sheer numbers of people will have stifled economic development and thwarted that breakthrough to a better life for all envisioned by her Five-Year Plans. Rather, she will remain deeply engulfed in the morass of poverty and misery.

But should births miraculously start to decline at once and continue downward to half their present level by 1981, India's high hopes for economic development may well be realized, even though her population would increase from nearly 400 million today to about 600 million by 1986.

[8] From "India: High Cost of High Fertility," by Robert C. Cook, editor of *Population Bulletin. Population Bulletin.* p 153-71. D. '58. Reprinted by permission. (This article is based on the work by Ansley J. Coale, and Edgar M. Hoover, entitled *Population Growth and Economic Development in Low-income Countries; a Case Study of India's Prospects.* Princeton University Press. Princeton, N.J. 1958.)

Should India's birth rate not begin to decline until 1966, an economic breakthrough might still be possible, but the delay would be costly in terms of postponed and more uncertain economic gains. . . .

The urgent necessity for a rapid reduction in India's birth rate is supported by considerable economic evidence. Briefly, it is difficult in an economically underdeveloped country like India to maintain a healthy balance between the need to save for investment in productive facilities on the one hand and, on the other, to meet the urgent necessity to spend for welfare and consumer goods and services, such as housing, education, health, food, clothing, etc. While outlays for productive facilities contribute directly to economic growth, outlays for welfare and consumer goods and services contribute only indirectly, if at all. . . .

During the fifty years prior to 1921, India's population increased by about 34 million. Since 1921, growth has been explosive—136 million in thirty-five years. At the current growth rate, 70 million will be added to the population in a decade. This does not represent maximum growth: the rate will accelerate as the death rate falls.

In this era of sanitation and public health programs, such population explosions happen in underdeveloped areas when high death rates are cut quickly—and cheaply. Birth rates tend to remain at traditionally high levels so population growth surges upward. This endangers any plans to achieve an economic breakthrough to higher living levels. . . .

India's death rate has been declining steadily since 1921. But her birth rate remains near its traditionally high level. . . .

India's population is now estimated to be about 400 million, with a yearly increase of almost 7 million. Unless India's birth rate starts to go down simultaneously with her death rate, the rate of growth will increase relentlessly.

Too Little Land

India has two fifths the land area of the United States and more than twice as many people. In fact, she has more people than the United States and the Soviet Union combined.

An agrarian, overpopulated country like India is at the mercy of the quality and extent of its crop area and of the elements. The productivity of her land is dependent on the monsoons, which govern the amount of food she can grow each year for her people.

One third of the people are concentrated on less than 6 per cent of the land. Population distribution is largely determined by topographic and climatic factors. . . .

The Curse of Pervasive Poverty

Like most other underdeveloped countries, the roots of India's endemic poverty lie in the fact that she is an agrarian country by tradition and culture. Yet she is unable to raise enough food for her rapidly growing population. By modern standards, India's agriculture is overcrowded with workers, unproductive, inefficient, primitive. She has relatively few industrial opportunities with which to siphon workers off the land.

Another great problem of Indian agriculture is the large number of people dependent upon it. In 1901, in the area corresponding to the Union of India, there were 146 million people dependent upon agriculture out of a total population of 235 million; in 1951, 250 million out of 357 million. In other words, there has been an increase of more than 100 million in the agricultural population without any substantial increase in cultivated land. Is it surprising, then, that agricultural conditions are much worse now than they were at the beginning of the century?

It is this increasing pressure of population upon the soil and the growing indebtedness of the farmers that have caused the emergence of a class of landless laborers and tenants. In 1901, they and their families included only 20 million persons; in 1951, they totaled 76 million, more than a fifth of the population. It is these people who are receptive to any political philosophy that offers them hope. They are pawns in the hands of all kinds of demagogues. . . .

The Challenge of the Century

The underdeveloped, overpopulated countries of the world are caught in a demographic squeeze as a result of the ever-increasing efficiency in controlling death rates. When this is considered in the context of the East-West struggle for leadership in Asia and Africa, the demographic dilemma of the agrarian countries has an added and sinister significance.

India's predicament is typical. Cultural mores are attuned to an earlier time when high mortality made all-out fertility essential. A low level of literacy tends to conserve these mores and prevent a rapid change in reproductive patterns. So the rapid decline in death rates ruthlessly accelerates the rate of population growth. . . .

The leadership of Asia in the years ahead could go to that nation which first comes to grips with the dilemma of too-rapid population growth. No other advance would give so great an impetus to economic development.

II. INDIA'S PROBLEMS AT HOME

EDITOR'S INTRODUCTION

It is easy to make a long list of staggering problems which India faces domestically—too high a birth rate, integration versus caste divisions, the difficulties of carrying out economic planning in a tradition-bound society, corruption in politics, the Communist threat, the need for rapid agricultural and industrial improvement, among others. These problems are dealt with in this section.

The first three articles in a sense provide the setting: an exploding population, still caste-ridden and with such great diversity that the communication on a national level of national purposes and goals is itself a critical problem. Birth control efforts now under way are discussed first; then the status of untouchables in India is outlined; and facts are given about India's masses which indicate how difficult it is to develop a nation-wide sense of purpose for India's planning goals.

In subsequent articles various authors deal with India's political scene, indicating that the dominant Congress party is experiencing great difficulties and may have more after Nehru's departure. The special problem of communism within India is also canvassed.

The concluding articles in this section deal with the nature of economic planning in India and the broad outlines of India's economic development to date.

PROGRAM FOR BIRTH CONTROL [1]

After years of delays, bitter disputes, false starts, incredible snarls of official red tape and interminable meetings, India has at last embarked on one of the most fateful experiments in human history—a nation-wide attempt to control skyrocketing population as a matter of formal governmental policy.

[1] From "Land of Too Many People," by Milton and Margaret Silverman, free-lance writers. *Saturday Evening Post.* p 25+. S. 19, '59. Reprinted by permission.

India is not the first overcrowded Oriental nation to turn to birth control. Since the end of World War II, Japan—once one of the world's highly prolific countries—has cut her birth rate in half. This reduction is not the result of widespread teaching of contraceptive methods, but has been brought about mainly by a large-scale program of extremely cheap, government-approved abortions, performed legally at the rate of 1.5 million a year for mothers claiming that bearing additional children would damage their health or cause them economic hardship.

"This is now war," says Lieutenant Colonel Bishen Lal Raina, the hard-driving army doctor who now runs India's family-planning project. "We cannot wait for perfect methods, or perfect plans, or the blessing of all the rest of the world. We must fight with the weapons we have. Perhaps now we may save India in time."

And time, he notes, is running out. India now has an estimated population of 400 million and a yearly increase of 6 million to 8 million. The world's leading authorities believe that this nation has scarcely one generation to put its house in order. A study made by Princeton University's Office of Population Research, with the support of the International Bank for Reconstruction and Development, forecasts that if India's birth rate continues at its present high levels that country will have a population of almost 800 million by 1986. In that event, experts believe, India will have passed the point of no return. The country's resources could not conceivably support such a population growth; inevitably, they think, the ancient land would collapse into a terrifying shambles of famine, disease and anarchy, perhaps carrying most of Asia along with it.

Three people have played key parts in getting the vast control program under way—Colonel Raina himself . . . ; R .A. Gopalaswami, an energetic and outspoken civil servant who has demonstrated his willingness to badger and battle everybody in or out of government to get action; and Lady Dhanvanthi Rama Rau, one of the best-known women of India, tall, gray-haired, charming, eloquent. . . .

During the past years, these three and their close associates have fought public and governmental apathy and inertia which would have driven weaker citizens to madness. . . .

In 1947, when India won its freedom from Britain, . . . the government was pledged to "lay stress on self-control, as well as to spread the knowledge of cheap and safe methods of birth control." But for four years essentially nothing happened.

"During the first years of our independence," the prime minister recalls, "we were terribly occupied with other matters—with the production of more food, with building more schools and more roads and more houses."

Under the direction of India's first minister of health, the distinguished Princess Amrit Kaur, daughter of the Raja of Kapurthala, about 145 birth-control clinics were opened, but were not operated actively. The health ministry was more occupied with malaria control; tuberculosis control and similar projects, all of which were important, but contributed to an even greater increase in population.

The 1951 census brought an abrupt shock. It revealed that even though the British had gone and India was managing her own affairs, the population was shooting up faster than ever. The help of the World Health Organization of the United Nations was sought, and the WHO promptly sent Dr. Abraham Stone, one of its top consultants who long had been prominent in the planned-parenthood movement. . . . But the American consultant soon found he would be strictly limited in his work in India.

Princess Amrit Kaur was a spinster, a respected member of the Church of England, and a firm believer in Mahatma Gandhi, whom she served as secretary for sixteen years. She made it clear the American would be expected to introduce only the rhythm or calendar method [of birth control].

Dr. Stone did his best. He set up teaching programs in two test areas and established a follow-up system. Finding that many village women were unable to count or had no access to a calendar, he adopted a "counting necklace," with the appropriate number of green beads to represent the "safe" days and red beads for the "unsafe" or "baby" days.

Whether or not the rhythm method had any real value in these trials is still a matter of debate. Some observers blame the lack of marked success on the general apathy of the villagers. A few doctors noted that the "counting necklace" was not being used according to plan. . . .

The 1951 census report also led to bitter attacks against the government for its lethargy, and demands for immediate action. One of the most vigorous critics was Lady Rama Rau, a member of one of India's most influential families—her husband formerly was Indian Ambassador to the United States—and generally regarded as the leader of India's family-planning movement.

As president of the All-India Family Planning Association, she opened fire on the government. She denounced the rhythm-method trial as a shocking waste of money and time. She called for establishment of thousands of birth-control clinics and for free contraceptives. She battled governmental red tape, internal jealousies, shortage of materials and general governmental inertia.

"You must realize," she says, "that the officials of my government surpass all others in the willingness to expend every effort to explain to you, with the utmost patience and tact, why anything which you might want—or anything which they might want—is totally impossible."

Owing in considerable part to her insistence, the government allocated about $1.3 billion for a national family-planning program under the first Five-Year Plan, from 1951 to 1956. Some of the funds were used to open about 150 family-planning clinics, a testing laboratory, the preparation of educational materials, and a variety of projects to investigate motivations and attitudes. Yet, by 1956, less than 75 per cent of the small first appropriation had been spent.

By 1957, however, it was generally agreed that the time for caution had passed. Princess Amrit Kaur retired as minister of health and was succeeded by the more aggressive D. P. Karmarkar. An enthusiastic army doctor, Lieutenant Colonel Bishen Lal Raina, was named Family Planning Officer, given an appropriation of about $10 million for the second Five-Year Plan, and promised more money if he needed it.

When he moved into his new job, Colonel Raina quickly laid
out a plan for local family-planning centers, fitting them into
existing health centers in each area wherever possible. "I want to
make this a part of regular health care," he said. "It is to be
entirely voluntary. Advice will be given only to those married
couples who ask for it. The views of those who object to family
planning will be scrupulously respected."

He repeatedly emphasized that the goal was "not to prevent
childbirth but to make it possible to bring up children in the
best and healthiest social climate."

To get a family-by-family program moving quickly, he called
for the training of 20,000 field workers and the establishment of
2500 family-planning centers by the summer of 1961. At present
more than 2370 teachers have been trained and are at work, and
more than 825 clinics have been established.

"We will have all the people we need for this program ready
and working within a year," he told me. "By then we plan to
reach at least 40 million families every twelve months. . . .

A radically different approach has been pushed by R. A.
Gopalaswami, a high-ranking member of the Indian civil service,
a trained mathematician, and the man who directed the eye-
opening 1951 cenus. "We are on the edge of disaster," he says.
"We cannot waste time with uncertain programs. The only
possible solution for us now is widespread surgical sterilization—
preferably sterilization of every parent with three or more
children."

In his 1951 census analysis he calculated that India's population could never be limited unless each family produced no more
than three children. "It makes no difference whether or not the
mother's health or the father's wealth can let the family afford
more than three children," he insists. "India cannot afford it."

Three years ago Gopalaswami was assigned to a new position
in Madras, in southern India. He discovered there that individual
physicians were already embarked on a modest program of
sterilization operations—a simple, fifteen-minute operation for
men, and a relatively simple operation for women which could be
done after childbirth. He promptly sent assistants to interview

patients who had undergone the operations and found that all were pleased with the results.

"That was enough for me," he said. "I went into action.". . .

All government hospitals in the state of Madras were ordered to perform the operations without charge. . . .

For the first year the Madras surgeons performed only a few dozen operations each month. Last year they were doing hundreds. By next year, Gopalaswami says, they will be doing thousands. In other parts of India doctors are following the lead of Madras and performing the sterilization operations in their clinics and hospitals. Still other surgeons have undertaken this work on their own. In the world-famed valley of Kashmir, for example, a group of surgeons—unaware of the Madras work —recently estimated that they have performed more than 10,000 sterilizations during the past five years.

As head of the family-planning project for India, Colonel Raina has approved sterilization as one effective method, but he has not gone overboard for it. "We will use whatever useful methods we can find," he says, "and we will continue to look for new ones."

Unquestionably, the most unusual new contraceptive under consideration is a pill, apparently effective when taken orally, which was developed by Dr. Sudhir Nath Sanyal, a physician working in a small, dark, overcrowded little private laboratory in Calcutta. . . . [Independent research by government scientists tends to confirm the effectiveness of these pills.—Ed.]

In New Delhi, Colonel Raina and his advisers feel the Sanyal pill still belongs in the experimental class, but they have approved further trials. . . .

"If the pills prove safe and effective under general village conditions," Colonel Raina says, "I will order them by the million and distribute them without charge."

Certain other Indian leaders are thinking along similar lines. Dr. H. J. Bhabha, India's world-famous atomic scientist, told a recent international conference that what India really needs is an "anti-fertility chemical" which could be added to the staple food —perhaps to salt, flour or sugar—and eaten every day. It would have to be highly safe, he said, but it would not have to be highly effective.

"If it would only reduce the statistical probability of pregnancy by about 30 per cent," he said, "our population growth would halt and our problem would be immediately solved."

Support for this proposal has come from such men as J. R. D. Tata, head of the huge Tata industrial empire and one of India's most vigorous industrial leaders. "Development of such a chemical would require a massive, intensive research program," he says. "This will be expensive, but we can well afford to buy such research."

Whether or not such an all-out research project will be undertaken, many American and European observers are beginning to believe that India may be on the way to solving its population problem. They note a growing sense of urgency throughout the whole government—a feeling that corners must be cut to get the job done before India's time runs out. Furthermore, many of them indicated that whatever happens in this country will have a tremendous effect throughout the rest of Asia, and in the overpopulated nations of Africa and Latin America.

THE UNTOUCHABLES OF INDIA [2]

Segregation, which in India is on a scale far vaster than in America, has been unconstitutional for ten years. But it is still flourishing. Attempts to abolish it still lead to violence. . . .[In 1957] an outbreak against untouchables in Madras raged for almost two weeks and brought death to more than forty persons. . . .

Large numbers of the 55 million untouchables—people who by tradition are looked down upon for reasons of their low birth—still find they must use separate water supplies, eat off different plates, live in separate communities. They have difficulty locating churches they can attend, have trouble sending

[2] From "Where 55 Million Are Segregated." *U.S. News & World Report.* 43:68+. O. 11, '57 Reprinted from *U.S. News & World Report,* an independent weekly news magazine published at Washington. Copyright 1957 United States News Publishing Corporation.

their children to school, and often are discriminated against for jobs. . . .

Those who try to treat untouchables as equals often find themselves in trouble. . . .

What the untouchables keep encountering is resistance that stems from more than three thousand years of deep-seated tradition. During that time an elaborate caste system has been built up in India. It is given sanction by the Hindu religion. At the bottom of all of India's 2,000 or more castes are the 55 million untouchables—born so low in the social scale that they are not even considered members of any caste at all.

Most Hindus firmly believe that contact with an untouchable means personal pollution. Even the path of his shadow is defiling. Untouchables pollute water and food, it is believed. They are not given access to Hindu temples. Usually they are forced to live in segregated districts. Only about 3 per cent of them—as compared with 15 per cent for all Indians—have ever had an opportunity to learn to read and write.

In recent years a great many educated Indians came to feel that untouchability was morally wrong and should be eliminated. By the time India became independent, the feeling was so strong that untouchability was made unconstitutional. Laws have provided fines and imprisonment for discriminating against untouchables and reserve to them 20 per cent of the seats in parliament and 12.5 per cent of all government jobs.

In addition, big sums have been spent to provide schools and housing for untouchables. The government has carried on a steady campaign of propaganda—through films, pamphlets, lectures and so on—to discourage untouchability among caste Hindus in the villages. Prime Minister Nehru has called outbreaks of violence against the disdained millions "terrible . . . primitive and foolish."

But all of this has barely made a dent. In most of India's 560,000 villages, untouchables are still segregated. They are restricted to the most menial jobs. Even in the cities, where they work in industrial plants, they often are forced to work in quarters separated from other Indians. At school their children are still required to sit on segregated benches.

There are many villages where untouchables are not allowed to enter residential neighborhoods occupied by caste Hindus, are not permitted to ride bicycles or wear certain kinds of clothing or use the public water supply. Often their only sources of water are the ponds where cattle are washed. They are forbidden to take the bodies of their dead through village streets.

The policy that 12.5 per cent of government jobs go to untouchables hasn't worked out in practice. For one thing, the educational level of most of them is so low they can't hold many jobs. For another, officials still tend to discriminate against them. In New Delhi, an untouchable who worked as an engineer in the public-works department—untouchables reaching this level of education are extremely rare—was passed over for promotion seven times.

Attempts to end school segregation haven't worked out, either. Some of the new schools opened up to untouchables now are attended only by untouchables. New hospitals for children are being run especially for untouchables. Reading rooms and even housing developments are being constructed for untouchables only.

The penalties called for by law for discriminating against untouchables are seldom invoked. A government report . . . [in 1956] said that throughout India only 297 cases were brought to court in a twelve-month period. The vast majority of untouchables either accept things as they are, or are too backward to know about their legal rights.

In past years, many untouchables have sought to change their status by leaving the Hindu religion and becoming Christians. A great number found, however, that being a Christian made no difference. They were still looked upon as untouchable by the people in their villages. Some find that, having renounced Hinduism, they are worse off than before.

Many educated untouchables are able to "cross the line" by moving into the larger cities and hiding their origins. But, in attempting to do this, the color of their skins—which is usually darker than that of other Indians—acts as a handicap. In general, the darker an Indian's skin is, the lower his caste is likely to be. The members of the highest caste, the Brahmans, usually have comparatively fair skins.

In choosing husbands and wives, Indians often place emphasis on color. Indians who advertise for wives in the columns of newspapers—an old Indian custom—frequently state their preference for fair-skinned brides.

Many Hindus will not permit their children to marry in a caste beneath theirs. Others will not eat at the same table with a lower-caste Hindu.

It is this type of tradition that has helped make it impossible to eliminate untouchability just by passing laws against it. This fact is now being admitted in Indian government publications and official reports—one of which says: "Any number of enactments by themselves will not transform the situation unless there is a genuine change of heart on the part of every . . . citizen."

Complete integration in India, it is now being recognized, is still a long way off, and the road toward it is studded with trouble and violence.

INDIA'S MASSES [3]

India is trying to build itself anew, and there are many visible signs of progress. But communications are still needed drastically. Only 18 per cent of the people in India can read and write. Two years ago a research team from Jamia Milia University in New Delhi surveyed 150 villages in selected areas of the four Hindi-speaking states of north-central India. They found that 6 out of 67 persons selected at random were entirely ignorant of the fact that the British no longer ruled India.

In response to another question, the researchers found that 54 out of 314 respondents did not know the name of their own country. Some, however, were aware of the word *Bharat* (India);

[3] From article by Arthur Bonner, correspondent in India. *Atlantic Monthly.* 204:48-51. O. '59. Reprinted by permission.

they said they had heard people shouting *Bharat Mata Ki Fai* (Long Live Mother India). But when these same villagers were asked what *Bharat* signified, they said they did not know.

It is difficult to try to communicate the complicated forms of modern democracy to a people who may not even visualize a nation. I accompanied Prime Minister Nehru shortly before a general election when he attempted just this. The Prime Minister visited the lovely old ruins of Mandu in central India, where five centuries ago there lived in a king who, with eight thousand wives, put Solomon to shame. A special effort had been made to gather together thousands of Gond tribesmen, who form the penniless peasantry of the surrounding scrub-jungle-covered hills. Nehru, speaking through a translator, gave a simple lecture in civics. He said there were no more British; they had all gone away. There were no more maharajas; they too were not ruling India. There were just the Indian people, who were ruling themselves. Everybody was an Indian, he said. He was an Indian and the Gonds were Indians. With no more British and no more maharajas, the Gonds like other Indians had the opportunity to choose who would be their rulers. He then went on to explain about the elections and what it meant to cast a vote.

Nehru was careful to speak slowly and to use simple terms that he repeated many times, as if speaking to children, but the entire idea must have been difficult for the Gonds to grasp. Nevertheless, Nehru delivers as many as a half dozen speeches a day during his tours because he knows that the only effective communication with the masses of India must be on a person-to-person basis.

The daily circulation of newspapers in India, with a population of 400 million, is only 3.1 million, and one third of these papers are in English. The dozen or so English-language papers are extremely important, since 99 per cent of the people are ruled by the one per cent who speak English. When I first came to India and heard people say this, I thought they were exaggerating. But my own experience has proved it true. I have talked to thousands of government officials and business, professional, and labor leaders throughout India, and we always conversed in English. An Indian who does not speak English cannot gain authority outside of his own limited circle. But the only persons who can afford the long education necessary to become proficient in English are those who were born with money or property. Thus the feudal system is perpetuated, and thus the English-language papers are so important; they help mold the opinion of the people who count.

But this should not be overemphasized. Newspapers have little impact even on many of those who are literate, either in English or the regional languages. Stanley and Ruth Freed are young American anthropologists who have spent more than a year working in a village only fourteen miles from Delhi. About two weeks after the revolt in Tibet began, when the Dalai Lama had just reached the Indian frontier, the Freeds asked several of the more educated people in the village what they thought of the matter. The newspapers were full of news about the Dalai Lama, yet only one of the persons the Freeds asked had even heard of him. The sole exception was a young man studying for his master's degree. Among those unaware of the Dalai Lama's existence was their interpreter, a young English-speaking girl who had completed two years of college.

There is no television in India, and there are only slightly more than 1.5 million radio sets in use, most of them in the four major cities: Delhi, Bombay, Calcutta, and Madras. The government has installed about 40,000 subsidized community radios in the villages, but this is just a beginning—there are 500,000 villages in India. It is more than just a matter of poverty. There are no repair facilities in the rural areas, and so an entire system has to be set up to keep the community radios in working order. Besides, many villages do not have electricity and need battery-operated sets, which means that the batteries must be brought into a district center at regular intervals to be recharged.

Language is a further barrier to understanding. There are fourteen major languages in India, plus a few hundred dialects, and when Nehru speaks in his native Hindustani he is understood by less than half of the people. Unfortunately, the intellectuals who run All India Radio, the government-owned radio network, scorn Hindustani as a polyglot tongue and insist on using a highly Sanskritized version of Hindustani called Hindi, which the government is trying to propagate as the national language. As a result, there are relatively few who understand the Hindi news broadcasts of AIR. The language pattern outside of north-central India is even more complicated. AIR news broadcasts in Bombay and Hyderabad are delivered in five languages, while special programs for the hill tracts of northeastern India are spoken in fifteen separate dialects.

It is laid down in the Indian constitution that the government should try to switch over from English to Hindi by 1965. But there is so much opposition to Hindi that the government recently had to promise that it would not insist on this deadline. It is not that those who oppose Hindi love English more, but they fear that if Hindi becomes the national language their own languages will be neglected. They also fear that those who speak Hindi as their mother tongue would find it easier to get government jobs than those who would have to learn Hindi as a second language. In most of the rest of the world language ties a nation together. In India language separates people and makes them enemies.

India is such a complex country that it needs modern communications to bind it together, yet a great majority of Indians live in the age of the bullock cart. The Indian Airlines Corporation, the government-owned airline that provides all of the internal passenger service and almost all of the air freight traffic, has only 77 aircraft on regular service. More than two thirds of these are decrepit DC-3's used during World War II. There are only 400,000 telephones, or one for every thousand persons. Most of the telephones, like most of the radios, are concentrated in the four major cities. There are only 110 pages in the telephone book for the entire state of Kerala, which has a population of 15 million, or almost double that of New York City. There is only one motor vehicle of any sort, including motorcycles, for every 850 persons. But there are 10 million bullock carts, or one for every 40 people.

Automobile drivers curse the bullock carts for slowing down traffic, and highway engineers hate them because their narrow, iron-rimmed wheels destroy the surface of the roads, especially in the summer, when the asphalt melts under the baking sun. Yet they are as much a part of Indian life today as they were at the dawn of Indian history. And, judging from ancient temple sculpture, the bullock cart has remained unchanged throughout the rise and fall of countless kingdoms. The cart has two wobbly wheels about five feet in diameter and is drawn by two humped bullocks with the yoke resting on the bullocks' necks in front of the hump and cutting into the flesh. The Indian peasant is poor in money and technology; the bullock cart is the only vehicle he can afford or knows how to use.

It is estimated that each bullock cart travels two thousand miles a year and that 70 per cent of the goods in India are carried by bullock cart. The 80 per cent of the Indians who live in villages are scattered as far as twenty miles from a motorable road. When the second Five Year Plan ends in 1961, there will still be but 138,000 miles of all-weather motorable roads, or one mile for every 9 square miles of territory. Only 1500 miles of this will be two-lane highways.

India depends primarily on its government-owned railroads for interregional movement. It has the fourth largest railroad system in the world, but it still does not meet India's needs. There are 35,000 miles of track, or 27 miles per 1000 square miles of territory, compared with 74 in the United States. There are only 9 miles of track per 100,000 people, compared with 138 in the United States. The Indian railroads were neglected during the depression in the 1930's. They were badly damaged and overworked in the war years and later when the subcontinent was partitioned between India and Pakistan. Meanwhile, population has increased at the rate of 7 million a year, and there is the new and heavy burden of the industries and projects begun under the two Five Year Plans. Because of all this, the Indian railroads today are less able to meet the demands made on them than they were thirty years ago, even though about 20 per cent of the Five Year Plan allocations are spent for railway improvement.

Traveling in an air-conditioned car on the Indian railways is about as comfortable as traveling Pullman in the United States, but third-class travel, which is what most Indians use, can be sheer horror. About two hundred passengers are jammed along with mountains of luggage into a single dirty, hot carriage. The seats are narrow and made of wooden slats. The smell of humanity is reinforced by the odor from the inadequate and seldom cleaned toilet. There is no drinking water on the train, and the rush for seats is so great that even when the train stops, a person who has a seat does not dare leave it to get a drink of water at the station. Some improvements have been made, but not many. The failure is deliberate. India is trying to build its industries, and freight gets priority over people.

Thanks to this priority, most of the outdated freight cars have been replaced and the total number has increased by 40,000 in the past ten years, but freight capacity is still inadequate. Businessmen complain that they have to wait three months for a freight car to carry their goods and that, at times, when a car is made available they have to wait another month before it can be attached to a passing train. They also complain that the movement of freight cars is so chaotic that even after goods are dispatched it might take a month for the shipment to arrive at a destination only five hundred miles away. The shortage of freight cars is a major cause of governmental corruption. Businessmen say that the only way they can get a car is by bribing railway officials.

Governmental inefficiency is the keynote. All of the interstate communications are owned by the central government, and many of the individual states have nationalized interurban bus and truck lines as well as their municipal transport systems. Yet entering a government office is like stepping back fifty years or more. There are few filing cabinets and paper clips. Papers are attached by a string threaded through a hole in one corner and then wrapped in a folder tied together by another string. A code letter is pinned to the cover, and the name of the file is registered in a ledger. The file is then tossed on a shelf along with mounds of others. The registers are tossed someplace else, and how any file is ever found again is a wonder. The rules for handling correspondence at the district level in Uttar Pradesh have changed little since they were drawn up in 1880. A letter has to pass through forty-one distinct steps and be entered in dozens of registers before it is answered. Throughout India, the government moves so slowly that it is not uncommon for an official to die before his pension is sanctioned and paid.

Fortunately, not all government organizations are so creaky. One of the most promising things in India is the Community Development program, which has shown itself receptive to new ideas and methods. It has sent thousands of village-level workers and others into the villages to teach everything from adult literacy to better ways of farming. It emphasizes the person-to-person approach and at times has shown great imagination. For instance, it has organized group tours of India by as many as five hundred villagers—tempting them with a chance to worship at the traditional shrines and, in the process, showing them the new factories and dams, which Nehru calls the modern places of pilgrimage. In trying to communicate ideas, the village-level workers have a whole armory of new weapons. All branches of the central and state governments are turning out books, pamphlets, and leaflets; special movies have been prepared along with audio-visual aids. There are hundreds of mobile vans equipped with generators to penetrate into the darkest interior, and there are even a few publicity setups mounted on bullock carts.

But an urban Indian intellectual is often as much a stranger to an Indian peasant as an Englishman or an American. Even when they do speak the same language, they do not think the same thoughts. When an educational movie is prepared in a Bombay studio, using actors disguised as farmers, the real farmers will always flock to the mobile van to see it. But they laugh at the wrong places. It is often a parody of their own lives and as such is entertainment, not education.

The problem is greater than just making more realistic films. Ideas not only have to be understood, they have to be accepted; and once accepted, they have to become permanent. The Community Development program works intensively in blocks of one hundred villages for about four years, after which the area is given much less attention. There are many apparent changes in these blocks. But Community Development officials have now found, much to their dismay, that the villagers quickly give up their new habits and ideas as soon as the external pressure is removed.

The reason for this is found in the word *dharma*, a religious term roughly meaning "the Hindu way of life." But since religion, especially in the villages, is intertwined with man's every act, it means more than the ceremonies of religion. Dharma includes all the ethics and mores of a man's family, caste, and community; it determines how a man dresses or plows his field or eats and even how he goes to the toilet. Dharma gives the sanction of heaven to the class and caste structure and lays down that superior authority must be obeyed. Thus a village-level worker, who represents authority, might easily get the peasant to change his habits. But once the village-level worker goes away, other aspects of the dharma—mainly the spiritual pressure of tradition—reassert themselves.

Foreign experts are often discouraged. I met a British nurse whom the World Health Organization had sent to Kerala, where she worked for three years establishing maternity and child-care centers. We had a long talk about all the things she had done, but as I got up to leave she remarked sadly that she would soon be going home and it would probably be forgotten. I also met an American who came to India under our technical assistance program. He was sent to an area where another expert a year previously had taught the villagers how to install and use a large number of diesel pumps for their wells. When the second man arrived at the scene, he found that none of the pumps were in use. Some were mechanically defective, others had simply run out of fuel.

Perhaps the best way of getting ideas permanently accepted would be to present them through religious channels. But Hinduism has no established church which can be used as a means of communication. There are only individuals like Vinoba Bhave, Gandhi's disciple, who is collecting thousands of acres of land as gifts for his Bhoodan movement. [See

"Problems for the Congress Party," in this section, below.]
Vinoba, with his asceticism and his long tours on foot, is operating within the dharma and is easily accepted. The landlords who
give part of their holdings to Vinoba for distribution among
the landless are the same men who strenuously resist all land
reforms proposed by the government. But the Westernized
administrators of India scorn Vinoba and his religion-oriented
methods.

Nehru often says that he is not "religious-minded," and
government spokesmen take pride in echoing that India is a
secular state. After living in India for more than five years
and realizing the force of the dharma, I am convinced that
there is a direct relation between the de-emphasis of religion
since Ghandi's death and the fact that much of the enthusiasm
that existed at the time of India's independence has now evap-
orated.

Many factories and huge new dams spring up, yet despite
the best efforts of the government, per-acre yields remain among
the lowest in the world, and thousands of ancient minor irrigation works are falling into disrepair. The level of literacy
is what it was a decade ago, and the fine-sounding laws banning
untouchability or child marriage are seldom enforced. That is,
there is a failure of the things that require the active cooperation
of the masses. This cannot be accounted for solely by the lack
of physical communications. Gandhi showed that despite the
absence of roads and post offices it is possible to establish contact with the vast masses and mobilize them for action. But
nowadays this spiritual rapport is missing; there is a vast gulf
between the rulers and the ruled. This has serious implications.
As long as there is no close contact between those at the top
and those at the bottom, democracy in India has slender roots.

PROBLEMS FOR THE CONGRESS PARTY [4]

India's Congress party is greatly in need of new and dynamic
leadership both in New Delhi and in the various states. A few

[4] From "Atlantic Report: India." *Atlantic Monthly.* 203:12+. Je. '59. Reprinted by permission.

months ago Prime Minister Nehru said "provincialism, casteism, and communalism" (religious rivalry) had developed within the party "to a scandalous and shameful degree." More than two years ago he admitted that the average Indian believes most Congress men are corrupt. Congress leaders themselves are responsible for this impression.

The party's executive committee recently censured five top leaders of Rajasthan for "setting a bad example," by issuing a joint statement accusing their chief minister, M. L. Sukhadia (roughly equivalent to an American governor), of "favoritism, nepotism, and corruption." But others had set the example earlier. . . . In 1958 dissidents within the Congress in Punjab drew up a 3000-word "charge sheet" accusing their chief minister, Sardar Pratap Singh Kairon, of the same things.

There are dissident cliques in every state. Some represent economic groups like big landlords. Others represent caste groups, and others regional groups. Sometimes an entire group breaks off. In Andhra recently twenty-seven Congress members of the state legislature resigned and are now trying to form their own party. A similar group broke away in Madras state two years ago and fought the last elections as the Congress Reform party. But experience has shown that splinter groups are ineffective. The cliques generally remain within the party, since this is the source of power and profit.

The 1957 Communist victory in Kerala was due primarily to feuding and mudslinging which destroyed the people's faith in the Congress party. . . .

Nehru used to spend a lot of time flying off to one or another of the state capitals to gather the feuding politicians behind closed doors and force them to patch up their troubles, at least temporarily. But it is growing obvious that Nehru's authority is waning. The party bosses in the states pay lip service to his calls for unity but openly continue their bickering, and the Prime Minister seldom even attempts to restore peace. Yet at the same time he holds most of the reins of power in his own hands, so that no one else is able to do what he is unwilling or unable to do.

Now even Nehru's personal reputation is being called into question. M. O. Mathai, the Prime Minister's special assistant, resigned following Communist charges that he had unexplained sources of income. The Communists want to know where Mathai got the money to buy a farm worth $25,000 and why leading industrialists contributed to a $225,000 trust fund in memory of Mathai's mother.

The Prime Minister has defended the integrity of his former special assistant and has flatly denied the implication that Mathai got money to influence his decisions. "I do not think it proper for anyone to imagine that Mr. Mathai influenced me in anything or in any policy," Nehru said.

Proper or not, the Communists have reiterated their charges. They demand a full, public inquiry, but Nehru has agreed only to a secret investigation by a single government official. This has given the Communists the chance to pose as the defenders of democracy. They have repeated their demands for an open investigation and say they will not lay whatever information they have before the secret group. "Mathais may come and go," declared Bhupesh Gupta, the Communist leader in the upper house of parliament, "but our parliamentary system and our democratic standards shall remain and we have to protect them."

Nehru's Popularity

No one believes that Nehru himself is involved in corruption, but the Mathai case does disclose several chinks in his armor. He is a poor judge of men. He is also impatient of implied criticism and either tries to ignore it or loses his temper and says harsh things to those around him. As a result there are few independent men around him, and there are fewer every year as the old stalwarts of the independence struggle— the men who knew Nehru as a youth and who make allowances for his moods—die off. They are replaced by others, who are at best yes men and at worst sycophants. . . .

Nehru is still the Congress party's greatest asset. . . . But the question is, what will the Congress party do for election material after he is gone? When Nehru's daughter, Indira

Gandhi (no relation to the Mahatma) was elected Congress president, she spoke of bringing younger elements to the fore and of instilling a new sense of discipline. A. S. Raju, a Congress general secretary, said her election would check a "drift toward the rightist trend of thought."

Her moves so far have been disappointing. The Old Guard members of the executive committee handed in their formal resignations so that she could appoint whomever she wished. She promptly reappointed almost all of the old bosses, explaining, "I cannot deprive myself of the sound and wise counsels of our national leaders in my attempt to make room for young blood." Nehru was dropped as a regular member of the executive committee but added as a "permanent special invitee."

How Much Socialism?

Nehru, contradictory person that he is, criticizes the Congress for its "provincialism, casteism, and communalism," but he also idealizes it. He once referred to the Congress as the "steel frame" of India, declaring that it was the only group which could hold the disparate elements of India together and at the same time provide democratic and socialist leadership. . . .

However, there are doubts whether the Congress really represents socialism. The term is misleading. Congress socialism is generally devoid of any ideological content; it means brotherhood, humanity, and a better deal for the underdog. The trouble with the Congress party is that its representatives sometimes belie its socialist slogans. . . .

The Poor Become Poorer

Out of a population of 400 million, 70 per cent are engaged in agriculture and allied pursuits. Of these, 30.4 per cent are without land or have so little land they are classified as agricultural laborers. They own one per cent of the land under cultivation and have a per capita income of $23 a year. Former Congress party president U. N. Dhebar admits that these agricultural laborers are "groaning under subhuman conditions."

Yet the Congress party, despite eleven years of majorities in most of the states of India, has not been able to bring about effective land reform. One has only to look at how some of these majorities were obtained to understand why.

The Congress barely got a majority in Orissa in 1957 but promptly strengthened itself by absorbing three men who had been elected on the feudalist Ganatanra Parishad ticket and by forming an alliance with the five members elected on the equally feudalist Jharkand ticket. These new Congress members and Congress allies have effectively sabotaged land reform measures, and the old Congress party members, who are interested in power more than principles, refuse to get rid of them.

Western visitors to India are always impressed by the many new factories and development works, but Indians themselves are more conscious of the fact that one third of the entire work force is either unemployed or underemployed. Mr. Dhebar has admitted that "the circle of the rich becoming richer and the poor becoming poorer remains unbroken." This is the sort of atmosphere that can destroy a political party or can even breed a revolution.

Bhave, India's New Gandhi?

Moreover, a new wind is stirring the countryside. Vinoba Bhave's Bhoodan (land gift) movement is gaining strength. It has collected more than four million acres, of which one million have been distributed and another million will be parceled out within a year. The rest is uncultivable. Bhave has also collected about 4500 villages as Gramdan—a plan whereby an entire village contributes all of its land to a common pool and farms it collectively. The Bhoodan movement aims at more than just land reform. Bhave wants a voluntary cooperative commonwealth built on a base of self-sufficient, self-administered villages.

To an American, Bhave's idea may seem too utopian to be practical. But India has its own traditions and ways of doing things, and Bhave is a product of these traditions. Thirty years ago much of what Gandhi said about how to oust the

British also seemed wildly impractical. Bhave has been able to convince several highly respected Indian leaders, including former Praja Socialist Jaya Prakash Narayan, of the validity of his approach.

Narayan was once believed to be Nehru's logical successor, but he renounced politics five years ago to join the Bhoodan movement. He is convinced that parliamentary democracy does not meet the needs of India's conditions. He thinks bossism, corruption, and feuds are almost automatic under the present system because it is too easy for a small, educated elite to take advantage of a vast, illiterate, and poverty-stricken peasantry.

Instead, he favors a series of indirect elections so that the peasants vote in small blocs for issues they can understand and for candidates they know personally. The persons elected from the bottom rung in turn vote for people to the next higher rung and so on up the line.

He also says the peasants must be given economic independence, and since there is not enough land for all, what there is should be worked cooperatively and the surplus labor used to produce most of a village's needs in clothing and small utensils and implements. Neither Bhave nor Narayan opposes large industries. They say that given the rapid population increase—now about 6 million a year—industries will never reduce the pressure on the land, so that capital-intensive heavy industries and labor-intensive cottage industries must develop side by side.

The Bhoodan ideas find ready acceptance among the Indian peasants. Bhave walks constantly, never stopping more than one night in any place. His march along narrow, dusty, back-country roads has taken on the proportions of a triumphal procession. The villagers come from miles around to greet him as he passes and then gather at his halting place to listen attentively to what he has to say.

Basically, Bhave is helping to spread democracy. He tells the peasants to rearrange their lives and lands without waiting for the government to act. He insists that no coercion be used. Although he does not preach anticommunism, he is actually a strong antidote to communism. If the Indian peasants can learn to handle their own village and district affairs and not succumb to violence, they will automatically learn how to exercise better control of their political representatives at the state level, and eventually at the national level. . . .

Ironically, although Bhave criticizes the Congress party for its obvious failings, there are usually a number of white Gandhi caps, signifying Congress workers, in his audience. Bhoodan is inspiring Congress district workers to become more active among the people. The old Gandhian idealism, which swept away the British, may again nourish the roots of the National Congress party.

COMMUNISM IN INDIA [5]

India had its first experiment with peaceful coexistence of Communist and non-Communist governments during the period, April 5, 1957, to July 31, 1959, within its own borders. With the fall of the Communist government of Kerala state, this experiment has been interrupted, if not terminated. New state elections were to be held at the end of 1959. This, then, is an appropriate occasion for assessing Communist policy in India.

Recent Strategy and Tactics

Current Soviet strategy in the underdeveloped countries may be compared to the "popular-front" policy in Europe during the years 1935-1939. Then it was "anti-Fascist," now it is "anti-imperialist" or, more specifically, anti-American. It is a strategy of mobilizing all "patriotic" forces within each country against the alleged threat of Western economic and military aggression. Applied to India, it is a strategy of collaboration with all groups of the population which support neutralism. Translated into tactics on the basis of India's circumstances, it means support of the "bourgeois" Nehru government so far as its actions are anti-Western in intent or in effect.

Within India the tactics of the Communist party (CPI) are to collaborate with all "democratic" parties and groups

[5] From "The Communists and India," by Gene D. Overstreet, professor of political science, Swarthmore College. *Foreign Policy Bulletin*. 39:29+. N. 1, '59. Reprinted by permission.

toward the goal of a "government of democratic unity," or a coalition government of Communist and non-Communist parties which have anti-imperialism and a diluted socialism in common. The CPI proclaims this goal both for each of the fourteen states composing the Republic of India and for the central government, but it concentrates on the state level of Indian politics. . . .

The Indian Communists tend to collaborate with Nehru's Congress government in New Delhi while attacking the Congress governments in the state capitols.

The main achievement of this policy, and its main test, is the Communist experience in Kerala state.

Communism in Kerala

The state of Kerala is one of the most politically disturbed regions of the Indian subcontinent. The state has a great variety of communal problems. There are unusually large Moslem and Catholic minorities, severe caste animosities, and an exceptionally large and dissatisfied intellectual minority. The resulting social tensions have produced a multiplication of political parties. The Congress, dominant nearly everywhere else, has been reduced to a minority party alongside the Praja Socialist party, the Revolutionary Socialist party, the Moslem League and the Communist party. Before 1957, parliamentary government in the state meant minority or coalition government, and it was inherently unstable. Until that year no government in Kerala (or, before the reorganization of states, in Travancore-Cochin) had held office for more than eighteen months. To cope with such instability, the central government, under the constitution, possesses emergency powers whereby in case of failure by a state government it can dissolve that government and administer the state by "presidential rule" until new elections. Between 1950 and 1957, presidential rule was declared on five occasions in India, and of these, two occurred in Kerala.

In the general elections of 1957 the Communists emerged as the largest bloc in Kerala's legislature. With the support of five independents whom they had helped to elect, they com-

manded an absolute majority and were thus able to form the
government, under Chief Minister E. M. S. Namboodiripad.
Confronted by the threat of New Delhi's intervention and by
a precarious electoral base, the Communists' natural course of
action was one of moderation. . . .

Moderate as the Communists were by their standards, the
effect of Communist rule was gradually to exacerbate communal and class differences. The Communists won an important
by-election in 1958, regarded as a test of their record, but
opposition increased. The potential strength of the opposition
is indicated by the fact that it controlled an overwhelming
majority of the newspapers and of the municipal and village
councils in the state. All that was needed was an issue which
would draw the lines for struggle.

The issue came with the government's Education Act, which
stated, among other things, that teachers in all schools receiving state subsidies, public and private, must be appointed
from a register maintained by the Public Service Commission.
Charging political intervention in education, the Catholic Church
announced its refusal to open parochial schools. This action
catalyzed the opposition, and soon all parties rallied against
the government.

Opposition to Education Act

At this point a crucial decision was made: the opposition
chose to resort to civil disobedience instead of awaiting electoral or judicial remedies. Under the aggressive leadership of
Mannath Padmanabhan, spokesman of the Nair caste, opposition groups joined in a campaign to paralyze the Communist
government and force either its resignation or its dissolution
by the central government. Demonstrations and riots occurred,
accompanied by police firings—not an uncommon event in
India. The campaign was to culminate on August 9, "Save
India Day," on which the opposition planned to undertake a
full-scale general strike avowedly aimed at eliminating the Communist government from Kerala and the Communist party from

India. (August 9, 1942, was the date of the Congress party's "Quit India" resolution against British rule.)

As "Save India Day" grew nearer, it became clear that no compromise was possible. The governor of Kerala and the Union President Rajendra Prasad recommended central action, and Nehru, at first reluctant, finally accepted it as necessary. On July 31 the Kerala government was dissolved. It retired quietly, and the local Communist protest was mild. . . .

Published reactions after the event were characterized by relief, accompanied by regret over the methods used in bringing down the Communists and gloom over the prospects in Kerala. . . .

Lessons of Kerala

Civil disobedience in Kerala was a bad precedent, not least because the Communists themselves are most likely to benefit from it. The CPI is best equipped, both by inclination and by organizational experience, to stage a similar civil disobedience campaign against a Congress state government. And shortly after New Delhi's takeover in Kerala it did precisely that in the traditionally turbulent state of West Bengal.

There are other potential benefits accruing to the CPI from the Kerala situation. Central intervention in state politics is generally unpopular, whatever the circumstances, and the prestige of the Congress may therefore be reduced both in Kerala and elsewhere in India. Moreover, given the circumstances of their fall, the Communists may evoke some sympathy by posing as martyrs. . . .

The result [of the next election] will depend on the ability of the opposition to remain united. But it is reasonable to expect that, whatever the result, the elections will contribute to further polarization in Indian politics. Whether the Communists win (in which case they would probably face a second downfall) or lose, they may tend to conclude that they cannot gain and hold power anywhere in India by parliamentary methods. Given their ideological bias, they may judge that a Communist government in India would have to fight for its life in a hostile environment, as Russia's infant Soviet government had to fight for its life in the "capitalist encirclement." They may conclude, in short, that peaceful coexistence of Communist and non-Communist governments is an impossibility within India. In that case, the CPI may be disposed to swerve from its hitherto peaceful path and resort to more direct action. [In the elections held in February 1960 the Communist party in Kerala was decisively defeated by an anti-Communist coalition.— Ed.]

Aims of World Communism

The future direction of Communist policy in India will, however, depend more on the interests and attitudes of international communism than on those of the Indian Communists.

Like the earlier anti-Fascist line, the anti-imperialist strategy is subject to abrupt change. Indeed, the conditions under which change could take place can be anticipated. The strategy would naturally be terminated with the defeat of the "imperialist" bloc, and, short of that, it would be less urgent if that bloc were relatively weakened. The Soviet leaders boast of the ability of the Communist states to overtake and surpass the West in the economic factors of power. As they grow more confident, may they not feel less need to collaborate with bourgeois allies with whom they share nothing but anti-imperialism? May they be less satisfied with the negative benefits of Indian neutralism, and more disposed to demand the positive benefits of Indian allegiance to the Communist bloc? . . .

More recently, and particularly since the fall of the Communist government in Kerala, the Chinese Communists have intensified their political and military pressures against border regions adjoining India and against India itself. However, this menacing situation may prove beneficial in terms of internal politics. Peiping's pressure on India has brought about a sharp split in India's Communist party, with some Communist leaders —among them Mr. Namboodiripad—declaring they are behind the Nehru government "for the defense of the integrity of the country and its freedom." [See articles in Section III below— Ed.]

PLANNING IN INDIA [6]

India's Five-Year Plans, their conception and magnitude, the resources and needs of the country, the difficulties in connection with foreign exchange, the desirability of foreign aid —all these and a number of related questions have received considerable attention in America. The extension of credit by the Export-Import Bank and the Development Loan Fund . . . [in 1958] was evidence of the desire of the U.S. government to make an effective contribution to India's economic development. The resolution introduced [in the U.S. Congress] by Senators John Kennedy and John Sherman Cooper (former U.S. Ambassador to India) for massive and coordinated support of India's plans and a strong plea by Senator Hubert Humphrey for large and sustained aid have served to make people increasingly aware of the importance of India's efforts for social and economic betterment. It is, therefore, essential to ask what is meant by India's planned development. Why is such a program necessary?

When India became an independent country eleven years ago, she faced enormous economic problems: a stagnant agricultural economy, an excessive population, woefully low standards of living, chronic unemployment and underemployment, lack of financial and technical resources. The lopsided nature of the economy was in no small measure due to retarded development under foreign rule. But the economic ills were also aggravated by postwar inflation and the after-effects of partition of the subcontinent.

On the other hand, the hopes for betterment of a people who had attained self-rule were understandably high. National freedom engendered "a revolution in expectations." Moreover, several projects for industrialization, power, and irrigation, and also programs for expansion of social services, had been formulated or were at various stages of implementation, and the necessity for some kind of coordinated effort for economic and social development was increasingly recognized.

* From "Can India Finance Her Five Year Plan?" by G. L. Mehta, former Indian Ambassador to the United States. *Atlantic Monthly.* 202:77-8+. O. '58. Reprinted by permission.

After the adoption of the constitution in India in January, 1950, a planning commission was set up to survey the whole economy and devise ways of mobilizing and augmenting the economic, technical, and human resources of the country. The commission is an advisory and consultative body and formulates its proposals and recommendations in close cooperation with various ministries of the union (federal) government and the state governments. It consults continually with various groups of men: industrialists, business and labor leaders, consumers, economic and technical experts, and legislators. India's plan is thus essentially democratic in its conception and execution.

No facile solutions or ready-made rules exist for the improvement of a vast, impoverished nation. The methods by which Western Europe and the United States progressed over a century and a half can have only a limited application in a country with a large and growing population which has no unconquered frontiers, no colonial territories. Countries like India have to seek their own answers to problems of agricultural reform and industrialization, the role of the state in an underdeveloped economy, the encouragement of private enterprise, and the guarantee of social justice. We are trying to do in India what it has taken centuries to achieve in the West.

India's plan is to build up a "socialist pattern of society." We need not be frightened of words, whether "socialism" or "capitalism." All civilized governments today seek for their people some kind of welfare state or society in which concerted efforts are made to improve standards of living, to provide an increasing degree of economic security, and to enlarge the scope of essential social services. In wartime the state performs many functions to attain common objectives and mobilize national efforts; countries like India are waging a war against poverty, unemployment, disease, and illiteracy, and have to make a similar endeavor. In this sense, as Sir William Harcourt, a former British Chancellor of the Exchequer, observed, "we are all socialists now."

The constitution of India itself has set forth the ideal of a welfare state based on social justice in which the ownership and the material resources of India are so distributed as to serve the common good and in which the economic system does not result in concentration of wealth and means of production to the common detriment. But a welfare state need not be a totalitarian state. The second Five-Year Plan has thus defined its objective:

The accent of the socialistic pattern is on the attainment of positive goals; the raising of living standards; the enlargement of opportunities for all; the promotion of enterprise among the disadvantaged class in the creation of a sense of partnership among all sections of India. These positive goals provide the criteria for basic decisions.

The government and people of India are seeking to achieve these objectives through consent, not coercion. Our people are using the polling booths, not barricades; constitutional processes, not dictatorial ukases.

Moreover, India's constitution lays down that there shall be no acquisition by the state without compensation, and wherever such compensation has been paid, as in the nationalization of life insurance companies or a gold mining industry, it has been not only fair but generous. Measures are adopted for economic reform after full debate and through parliamentary procedures. In the Indian economy, agriculture, consisting of privately owned farms, is the predominant industry. No program is visualized for collectivization of the land; the emphasis is on development through cooperatives. While feudal estates are being broken up so as to make the tiller the owner of the soil, ceilings are provided for holdings of land in several states.

Private enterprise contributes nearly 98 per cent of the total industrial production, and it is actively encouraged by the state in its expansion. Thus, two private steel plants have been assisted in their schemes for doubling their capacity through governmental guarantee from World Bank loans, even though three government steel plants are being set up. In other words, the government is willing to help to achieve the maximum national product through private enterprise as well as through state-owned and -managed industries and services. The Indian people constantly remind themselves that the individual on the farm and in the factory is at the center of national development. We believe that a plan is for man, not man for plan.

During the period of the first Five-Year Plan (1951-1956) the spell of stagnation was broken. The national income increased by 18 per cent and the per capita income by 11 per cent, taking into account the growth of population. The output of food grains went up by nearly a fourth, or by 11 million tons, and agricultural production as a whole by 19 per cent. Through irrigation and land reclamation the area under crops increased by 26 million new acres.

Nearly 80 million people comprising one fourth of the rural population felt the impact of a dynamic community development program. This program is designed to revivify rural life by improving productivity and providing employment through rural industries. It also aims at improving the health, education, and communications in the village areas. A useful yardstick for measuring the success of such projects is the extent of voluntary contributions of the people; nearly half of the expenditure of this program has been made through voluntary contributions by villagers, in the form of free labor, materials, land, and even cash. A silent revolution is spreading through the countryside. On its success depend the stability and progress of a land where 80 per cent of the people live in villages.

Along with agricultural progress, industrial production increased by 30 per cent by the end of the first plan. Employment was provided for nearly 4 million more people; 6 million more children went to primary schools; the number of technical institutes and universities grew steadily; and health services were extended. But the success of the plan has to be judged not merely in terms of physical targets and percentages of increase in production and consumption, important as they are for an economically backward country. What is more vital is the creation of a new spirit of enthusiasm, hope, and confidence. This the first plan, in a large measure, achieved.

Unfortunately, it did not make an adequate impact on the economy. A start had undoubtedly been made, but it was recognized that future development had to be more basic as well as speedier. The second Five-Year Plan, therefore, is essentially an attempt to lay the foundations of sustained development. Briefly, its objective is to obtain a 25 per cent increase in national income—from $21 billion in 1955-1956 to $26 billion in 1961. Production of consumers' goods is expected to rise by 21 per cent, with the balance plowed back into national development projects. In terms of per capita income the increase expected is 18 per cent, but in concrete terms this increase can hardly be regarded as ambitious. It would increase the per capita income from fifty-six dollars a year to sixty-six dollars. The ratio of investment to national income would go up from 7.3 per cent to 11 per cent, which is still low in comparison with that of many countries. Employment opportunities are to be provided for an additional 6.5 million people. Food production is to be increased by 25 per cent. Manufacture of steel, which is basic to the Indian economy, would rise to 4.5 million tons a year, which is quite a modest target for a population of 380 million people. [Targets of the second Five-Year Plan have since been cut back to a "hard core" program.—Ed.]

But with all the industrialization that is envisaged, India is and will remain a predominantly agricultural country. To bring and conserve water for Indian farms, to supply fertilizer and manure to Indian farmers, to adopt more efficient practices in consonance with local conditions, organize the farmers for cooperative action, provide schools and health clinics, supply light and power to rural homes and industries, and develop better communications and transport—these are the primary tasks which the government is undertaking. We recognize that India cannot be prosperous unless her villages are improved; but the countryside will not be in a healthy state until the national economy is further diversified, the pressure of population on the land is reduced, avenues of employment extended, and industry built up.

This second plan has run into difficulties in regard to foreign exchange resources available for import of food grains, capital goods, and industrial raw materials. Therefore, the criticism is leveled that the plan has been "overambitious." It has undoubtedly set high targets for production of food and industrial goods and for increasing incomes and social services. But the country cannot attempt less under the intensive pressure of a rapidly increasing population and of insistent public expectations and demands. It should also be pointed out that difficulties in regard to foreign exchange have not been due to the importation of luxuries or misdirection of scarce resources; by and large, the money has been expended on productive and remunerative projects.

In implementing plans of development, India has received a substantial amount of foreign aid from the United States, from the Colombo Plan, and from other countries, including Soviet Russia. The foreign aid received, however, constituted only about 10 per cent of the total developmental expenditure. The principal financial burden has been borne by the people of the country themselves. India is probably the highest taxed country in the world relative to capacity. . . .

A national plan is not merely an inventory of schemes and projects; it must be bold in order to stimulate effort, inculcate initiative, strengthen creative forces. And the people must feel that despite all difficulties and obstacles their government is making a maximum effort for their welfare and progress. "Against the danger of a big plan," Professor J. K. Galbraith observed after a visit to India and study of her plans, "must be set even greater dangers of frustration of the democratic spirit which would follow from one that seemed reluctant, inadequate, or even insufficiently bold." In balancing the risks, we have to take into account the prevalence of chronic unemployment with its maladjustments, waste, and social discontent. These are facts which a realistic democratic government has to face. . . .

NEEDED: MORE FOOD [7]

India is facing a crisis in food production. More specifically, it is a crisis in food-grain production because food grains comprise two-thirds of the caloric intake of the average Indian. The

[7] From "India Racing to Feed 480 Million by 1966." *Economic World.* 1:6. My. '59. This article quotes from the conclusions of "Report on India's Food Crisis and Steps to Meet It," by an agricultural reporting team sponsored by the Ford Foundation, published April 1959 by the government of India.

crux of the problem is food enough for the rapidly increasing population.

Five million persons per year were added during the first Five-Year Plan, and seven million per year will have been added during the second plan period. Ten million per year probably will be added during the period of the third plan ending in 1966. Although there is considerable emphasis on family planning in India, no appreciable slowing down of population growth may be expected during the third plan period.

This means that food will have to be provided for 80 million more people by the end of the third plan. This explosive increase in population will raise the total from 360 million in 1951 to an estimated 480 million by 1966.

Substantial expansion of food-grain production is necessary even to maintain existing consumption levels, which are among the lowest in the world. The present population places severe pressure on food supplies, and unfavorable crop conditions create an immediate crisis.

The successive Five-Year Plans have included food-grain production targets as major components. . . The first plan set a target of 65.5 million tons by 1955-1956. This target was achieved quite easily as a result of greater emphasis on agricultural production, and with the help of favorable weather.

The second Five-Year Plan set a target of 80.5 million tons of food (including legumes) grains by 1960-1961. But the annual crop returns are less than the target rates.

. . . Preliminary planning is now under way for the third plan. No specific targets have been announced, but discussions indicate that from 100 to 110 million tons of food grains will be required by 1965-1966. This assumes that population will continue to increase at projected rates, and that a small rise will continue to take place in per capita consumption of food grains.

A target of 100 million tons would permit a net daily consumption per person of 15 ounces of cereals and 3 ounces of pulses (legumes) for the prospective population. This compares with the consumption in 1956-1957 of 13.3 ounces of cereals and 2.4 ounces of pulses. A target at this level, therefore, would allow for some improvement in the diets of those who are now at bare subsistence levels, but it would not provide a safety margin for adverse weather nor for reserve stocks needed to stabilize prices and to meet other unforeseen emergencies. A target of 110 million tons is necessary to allow for these contingencies.

In addition to food-grain production, any balanced agricultural program should provide also for additional production of dairy and poultry products, fruits and vegetables to meet the demands of an expanding urban population and to permit gradual improvement in diets.

But the conclusion is clear: the gap between needs for food grains, as indicated by the plan targets, and supply, as indicated by production trends, is growing wider. The relatively favorable 1958-1959 season failed to reach the annual average of the food-grain target by 4.3 million tons, and the 1957-1958 crop was 9.3 million tons short. If food-grain production increases no faster than indicated by the present trend, the gap between supply and needs in 1965-1966 will be about 28 million tons.

In order to produce 110 million tons of food grains annually by the end of the third plan, the rate of production increase must average 8.2 per cent per year for the next 7 years. This rate of increase compares with an annual average of 2.3 per cent from 1949-1950 to 1958-1959, and an average of 3.2 per cent from 1952-1953 to 1958-1959. The task is overwhelming. The urgency of an all-out effort is obvious. Adequate resources must be made available to accomplish the job.

It is clear that the necessity for conserving foreign exchange requires holding imports of food grains to a minimum level, except as imports become available under special exchange programs. In any case, no conceivable program of imports or rationing could meet a crisis of this magnitude.

A third plan target of 110 million tons must be reached if the country is to go forward on its development program. In fact greatly accelerated expansion of food production is necessary to prevent hunger and possible civil disturbance.

This target can be achieved if an all-out emergency food production program is undertaken. The best in Indian agriculture is comparable to the best in other countries, but the average level is unduly low. The task before the country is to develop ways of raising the low average to the higher levels that many Indian cultivators have achieved.

THE SILENT REVOLUTION [8]

In India—as in most of the less developed world—some four out of every five people live in rural villages or on farms.

And in India, that means well over 300 million people— and some 200,000 villages.

This suggests something of the vast scope of the current programs which India started from scratch in 1952 and which aim to establish community development projects or rural extension services throughout the land by the end of the second Five-Year Plan in 1961.

It also suggests why the Community Development Program has been called "the silent revolution."

On Mahatma Gandhi's birthday anniversary—October 2, 1952—India entered upon the first stage of community development with fifty-five selected pilot projects, each project covering an area of about 500 square miles and including some 300 villages.

Since then the program has expanded rapidly on two fronts: the National Extension Service and the Community Projects Program. The first provides minimal basic services and a modicum of financial assistance to permit local groups to get started on small-scale programs of rural improvement. The second is a series of rounded programs designed to raise standards in agriculture, health and sanitation, education, housing, communication, women's welfare, and cottage and small-scale industry. As areas covered by the National Extension Service begin to make progress, they move into the more intensive Community Development Program. The ultimate goal is to extend full-scale community development programs to all of rural India.

Underlying the entire program are the principles of self-help and mutual help. As projects are worked out in each

[8] From article in *Economic World*. 1:A-3. My. '59.

area, the local communities qualify for assistance by meeting an agreed scale of voluntary contributions in money, in kind, or in labor. Publicly-provided financial assistance is shared by the central and state governments. For wealth-producing projects, such as irrigation works, funds are advanced by the central government to the state governments in the form of interest bearing loans.

And heavy emphasis is placed on the stimulation of local initiative and action through local institutions like the *panchayats* . . . [village councils].

By the end of the first Five-Year Plan in 1956 the interim goal of the Community Development Program had been reached.

One fourth of the entire rural population had been brought within the orbit of the program. Some 80 million people were involved in community improvement programs. Here are some of the results by mid-1957:

Some 150,000 community centers had been started.

Nearly 4,000 primary health centers had been established.

More than 1,200 maternity and child welfare centers had been created.

Some 70,000 adult education centers were in operation and nearly 2 million adults had been made literate.

About 25,000 new schools had been built and 10,000 more converted.

Nearly 3,500 production and training centers for arts and crafts had been established.

Village housing projects were under way in 500 villages.

And nearly 60,000 cooperative societies had been formed.

Priority activities included the improvement of village wells, the extension of fruit and vegetable cultivation, the use of improved seeds and fertilizers, the upgrading of animal and poultry stocks, the construction of roads, and the drainage of land.

And for every dollar of contribution by the government, the rural people contributed the equivalent of sixty-one cents.

The United States—among other countries—has cooperated and provided a measure of assistance to India in the conduct of its "silent revolution." Over a period of about six years, some $15 million has been made available from Technical Co-operation funds. U.S. agricultural extension experts have helped develop study courses and demonstration projects. From the beginning the Ford Foundation has helped to train thousands of community development workers and has supported fifteen pilot projects in rural development.

Under the second Five-Year Plan, India has quadrupled the resources allocated to the Community Development Program —and established the goal of reaching the entire rural population with either the National Extension Service or with full-blown Community Development Programs. This will require the expansion of National Extension Service areas from 500 to 3,800 and the number of Community Development areas from 622 to 1,120.

Community development throughout the free world seeks to build economic and social progress on the traditional values and institutions of rural societies.

India today is conducting the world's largest program of rural community development.

And observers agree that its success or failure has significance for all of Asia and beyond—for throughout the less developed world the Indian program stands in stark contrast to the commune system of Communist China.

III. INDIA'S PROBLEMS ABROAD

EDITOR'S INTRODUCTION

Americans know more about Indian attitudes on foreign affairs—which they have sometimes criticized severely—than they do about India's internal aims and problems. Interest in India's foreign policies has been heightened because of the recent India-Red China border dispute.

Currently Prime Minister Nehru and other Indian foreign affairs spokesmen reaffirm that India's policy is that of non-alignment in the cold war. And Nehru has exercised great caution in dealing with Red China's aggression across his country's northern frontiers. Yet it is obvious that new attitudes toward Red China and the cold war are emerging in India. Much of the Indian press is critical of the government's extreme caution in responding to Red China's action.

Adequate analysis of these very recent changes in Indian attitudes on foreign affairs is not yet available. The first article below sets forth views on Indian foreign policy as of 1956. Many of these attitudes and policies still persist. Next, an article on Indian views on disarmament, followed by Nehru's statement on his nonalignment policy made only weeks before the Tibet crisis.

Then the Kashmir problem is dealt with as of 1957. This was the most crucial foreign policy issue India faced before the present attacks by Red China. But India's relations with Pakistan are also undergoing change, not least because of Communist pressure from the north. Recently frontier disputes between these two nations have been settled; in addition significant progress is now being made in resolving a dispute over the joint India-Pakistan use of the Indus River waters on India's western border. Some experts now believe that the Kashmir problem itself may become less difficult to settle.

Indian-Red Chinese differences are of a wholly different scope and directly involve New Delhi in a dispute with one of the chief Communist powers in the cold war—just the kind of situation Nehru has done his best to avert in conducting his nation's foreign policies. By suppressing the revolt in Tibet, Peiping alerted India as never before to the dangers of the policy of "peaceful coexistence" with the Communist world which India has promoted. Nehru's reaction to the Tibetan take-over is given in a statement made in the Indian parliament.

The next few articles attempt to throw some light on new Indian attitudes toward Red China and on the latter's reasons for violating India's northern frontiers.

INDIA IN THE COLD WAR [1]

The "peaceful competition" between Russia and the United States—to put it less fashionably, it is the "cold war" again—is producing a prime case history here. The results so far are deeply disturbing for the West. A combination of Soviet adaptability, American clumsiness and Indian shortsightedness has built up in the minds of scores of millions of people a mental image of the world that goes something like this:

"The United States, for all its talk about peace, would like to destroy the Soviet Union by war. The only thing holding it back is the fear of dying itself under Russian hydrogen bombs. Many important American leaders think the United States can destroy without being destroyed and some day may try.

"That is why the United States, in spite of talk about freedom and the American revolutionary heritage, is interested in the independence movements of the world only so far as they affect the fight against the Soviets. That is why the United States is the friend of the colonial powers.

"The Soviet Union is trying to walk the road of peace. It is a dictatorship but part of the fault lies in the fact that the Western powers have surrounded it with enemies since its birth. Give the Soviet Union a period of freedom from fear and the dictatorship will relax. In the meantime, Moscow supports the freedom struggles of the colonized peoples and fights for peace."

[1] From "India: a Case History in the 'Cold War,'" by A. M. Rosenthal, Times correspondent. New York Times Magazine. p 9+. F. 5, '56. Reprinted by permission.

Not everybody in India feels this way but the preceding three paragraphs are quite close to the picture of the world that is painted across the country—and in much of Asia. And the number of people who would substitute the Soviet Union for the United States in the foregoing is becoming fewer.

This is not just a lot of Communist talk either. The trend is shown in the results . . . of India's first major public opinion poll, taken in West Bengal. Only 7 per cent of the people questioned said that they would vote Communist. But 31 per cent said they thought the United States was preparing for an aggressive war. Only 2 per cent were afraid of the Soviet Union.

Put statistics aside. A foreigner staying any length of time in a country gets its political "feel." Sometimes that's a good deal more important than polls and figures.

In India the "feel" is not one of hatred, not even of dislike. If it were it would be simpler. Your political nerve ends tell you as you travel around India that you are not among enemies but among people, who to their own unhappiness, are beginning to distrust the motives of your country, who do not see your country as you see it. . . .

The poll in West Bengal showed that a shockingly large percentage of the people thought of us as warmongers. But that suspicion was just one ingredient in a compound of fears and misunderstandings. It does no good to try to isolate that one ingredient in this awful prescription for doubt and concentrate on it. The other elements in the compound act on the war-mongering fear and build it up.

The suspicion in India that does the United States the most harm is that we can no longer be counted on as friends of the independence movements. The belief is that we have abandoned the anticolonial peoples in favor of what we take to be our military security. . . .

In India, a short statement by [the late] Secretary of State Dulles about the Portuguese possessions of Goa on India's west coast did the United States as much word-for-word harm as any declaration ever made. All Dulles did was to speak of Goa as a Portuguese "province." To Indians that meant he was recognizing

Lisbon's claim that the little colony on the Arabian Sea was an inseparable part of Portugal.

The worst of the Dulles statement was that it cut the ground from under many Indians friendly to the United States. Suddenly they found themselves defending a country that had taken a stand involving their own patriotism. The bitterest reaction to Dulles' statement came from our closest friends in India.

The contrast that is built up when the Russians enter the picture is obvious. Where we give explanations, they give support. Free Goa. Free North Africa. Free everybody—except of course a few hundred million people in certain parts of the world not often mentioned hereabout.

Certainly the politically sophisticated of India know that the Soviet Union's display of affection for peoples of colonial areas has more behind it than uncontrollable brotherly love. But they believe, too, that because the Soviet Union's support of independence movements in public puts more pressure on the ruling powers, this brings the day of freedom that much nearer. And they think that, when the day comes, the new nations, given the right support by the West will not turn toward Moscow.

This is part of the picture—the fact that the United States is counted so often on the wrong side of the colonial fence. And part of the rest is that so many Indians think our entire international policy, unchecked, could lead to world atomic war. India feels that our refusal to recognize Communist China is the prime cause of tension in the Far East. The idea that we would have been willing to go to war, as Dulles . . . indicated, to defend the islands of Quemoy and Matsu, is one that horrified Indians. They think that we have become almost insanely casual about threatening to use atomic bombs. . . .

In the Indian attitude toward the United States there are two other elements. One is Pakistan. Scratch an Indian on foreign policy and you find deep emotional resentment at the fact that we are giving arms to India's neighbor. The Indians feel that the Pakistanis are taking United States arms to prepare themselves not against the Russians but against India.

Both nations try to avoid war, but both nations know the possibility of it always exists. A country that gives large-scale arms aid to one side must expect at least coolness from the people of the other. Whether it comes to pass or not, the Indians cannot ignore the possibility that American tanks and American artillery may some day be used against Indian troops.

The other element is color. Old-timers among Westerners in India tell each other that that's what all the fuss is about when you get right down to it. "They're brown and you're white and don't think your best friend in India ever forgets it."

The year this reporter has spent in India has not taught him enough to know whether the color resentment is all that deep and ineradicable. But it has taught him that it exists and that in any political assessment it is best to recognize that it exists.

It exists as between Indians themselves. . . .

It exists as between Indians and the foreigner. At a dinner party one of the high officials of the Indian government was talking about books and art and how, of course, he was really a Westerner in upbringing. Then he thought a brief moment and said, "Even though I am sure you find that hard to believe because my skin is dark."

The sensitivity to color cannot be pinned down on statistical tables. But it is not simply a negative matter of resentment against discrimination. It has become a positive thing, and so far it has benefited the Communists. There is something satisfying to Asians about the idea of a non-white country such as Communist China being powerful to the point where the Far Eastern policy of every "white" country in the world must center on her.

India's self-consciousness about color has not seemed to apply to the Soviet Union. One reason may be Russia's alliance with Communist China and her steady propaganda that under communism peoples of different races have learned to live together. But more important is the fact that resentment about color naturally turns against the West because it was the West that colonized Asia, ruled as the master and set up the "European only" curbs.

As for the United States, it suffers heavily in Asia because of discrimination against the Negro. It may be logical to point out that the Indians themselves have a social color line against people of darker skins in their country or that the communal riots here take thousands more lives than all Southern lynching parties put together. It may be logical—but attitudes on color are not built on logic.

These, then, are the things that make for suspicion and coldness toward the United States—a cloudy policy on colonialism, too much big talk about the diplomatic powers of the atomic bomb, a system of military alliances that strengthens Pakistan, and color.

And then there is India's contribution .

A nation's neutrality depends on two things: whether she considers herself neutral and whether the rest of the world considers her neutral. India considers herself neutral. . . .

By tradition and emotional make-up Nehru is the antithesis of a totalitarian. In a Communist world he would be one of the first marked for death. At home he denounces Communists. In Bombay during the riots Communists were thrown into jail. He attacks the Indian Communists as slaves of the Russians. And yet he builds a handsome image of the masters for the Indian people to look at. . . .

There is more than one reason why Nehru seems to be so much more concerned with Soviet sensibilities than with Western sensibilities. Nehru thinks that given a period of relaxation internationally the nature of the Soviet dictatorship will change. He thinks the Russian people are now at a point where they can keep their Communist economic system going under a government that gives them civil liberties.

And it is not surprising at all that Nehru welcomes the support of the Russians on India's two most emotional controversies—Goa and Kashmir. It seems to have become the thing to do to take help where you can find it. The United States counts among its allies Spain and dictatorships in Latin America and the Middle East. Washington never got perturbed about the iron-handed rule of the Afghan government until the flirtation with Moscow began.

It is also quite clear that Nehru feels our foreign policy comes not only to the verge of war but to the verge of madness.

But the fact still is that what India is doing is against her own interests as well as ours. It is probable that the essential Soviet game these days is to isolate India from the West. To the extent that India cooperates by hammering us and hugging the Russians she works against her own interests. . . .

The emphasis on India's responsibility is not for the sake of recrimination. India has made a place for herself in the world. It is an adult world and adults have responsibilities to one another.

There is no point in shrieking at India. She is entitled to her way and her thoughts. But the Western powers have a right to expect one thing from India—that she makes sure her people see the world not through a distorted and clouded glass, but as it really is.

INDIAN ATTITUDES ON DISARMAMENT [2]

Throughout Asia feeling against the manufacture, use, or testing of nuclear weapons runs noticeably high. Pending agreement by the nuclear powers on the comprehensive control of nuclear weapons, many Asian people and nations have focused their efforts on bringing about a cessation of nuclear-weapons tests.

This deep concern about nuclear weapons has its roots in several factors. One of these is that the only employment of nuclear weapons in wartime occurred against Asian people—the inhabitants of Hiroshima and Nagasaki. In Japan, in particular, the memories and scars of the atomic bombs dropped at Hiroshima and Nagasaki have accentuated the fear of nuclear warfare.

A second important factor is that most of the tests of large nuclear weapons apparently have taken place in the Asian and Pacific area. The usual Soviet proving ground is located in southwest Siberia, north of India, Afghanistan, and Pakistan, and west of China; the United States has tested its largest weapons in the Pacific islands under its trusteeship; and the third state which has tested nuclear weapons, the United Kingdom, has

[2] From *Control and Reduction of Armaments—Disarmament and Security in Eastern and Southern Asia*, staff study no 9 of the Subcommittee on Disarmament. United States Senate. Committee on Foreign Relations. Supt. of Docs. Washington, D.C. '57. p 21-4.

done so in the Australian area and near Christmas Island in the Central Pacific. Prime Minister Nehru of India has stated:

"It is of great concern to us that Asia and her peoples appear to be always nearer these occurrences and experiments and their fearsome consequences, actual and potential."

When, in spite of precautions, a nuclear-weapon test did cause personal injury and economic loss, as in the case of the Bikini explosion of March 1, 1954, it was Japanese fishermen and Marshall Islanders who suffered the results. After recent Soviet tests the radioactivity of the atmosphere became so high that the Japanese government warned that water should be boiled and vegetables washed carefully to make sure they were decontaminated.

Many of the Asian countries have demonstrated their reaction to the continuation of nuclear-weapon tests. The final communiqué of the Conference of Asian-African nations at Bandung in 1955 declared:

"Pending the total prohibition of the manufacture of nuclear and thermonuclear weapons, this Conference appealed to all the powers concerned to reach agreement to suspend experiments with such weapons." . . .

Several proposals have been made by Asian states on the limitation of nuclear tests. India in 1954 proposed a "standstill agreement" on nuclear explosions which it has frequently reiterated. Premier Nehru recently suggested to the Asian Legal Consultative Committee that it examine how far nuclear-weapon tests conform to international law. . . .

Since the end of World War II the Soviet Union on numerous occasions has proposed the liquidation of bases on the territory of other states. India, too, as part of its opposition to military alliances has condemned the maintenance of bases on foreign soil. In the Asian-Pacific area adoption of these proposals would affect the United States almost exclusively. American military, air, and naval bases are locted in Japan, Korea, and the Philippines, as well as Okinawa. Termination of these bases would necessitate the withdrawal of the forward line of American defense hundreds of miles to Alaska, Guam, the Pacific Trust Territory, and the Hawaiian Islands. Some British bases, for instance those in

Pakistan, and Malaya when it becomes independent, might also be construed as being located on "foreign" territory. Soviet Russian and Chinese Communist bases in Asia are all on their own territory and thus would be unaffected by this proposal, except that the Chinese Communist forces based in North Korea would have to retreat behind the Yalu River boundary line between Korea and China.

Although the United States has consistently rejected proposals for dismantling foreign bases, under certain conditions American bases could be negotiable. If the political and military conditions that originally necessitated establishment of the bases are changed, for instance, if outstanding political problems such as those of Korea, Taiwan, and Vietnam were settled, or if the perfecting of long-range missiles or aircraft made overseas bases less necessary, then the feasibility of negotiating a withdrawal would be enhanced. One prerequisite to any agreement on overseas bases in Asia, however, would be the necessity of obtaining from the Communist states a *quid pro quo* that would match in strategic value the concession made by the United States in withdrawing from its western Pacific positions.

INDIA'S NONALIGNMENT POLICY [3]

What we have sought to do is to follow a policy which seems to us to be correct both in regard to our own interests, short-range and long-range, but also which helps somewhat in serving the very broad cause we have in the world, the cause of peace.

Originally there was . . . doubt that the way India functioned was somewhat different from the way other countries functioned, not because we did not join these big military blocs—other countries also did not join the military blocs—but because there was a slight but significant difference in our approach to problems or rather in the way we expressed ourselves in regard to problems, a difference which was no great virtue in us but which came to us because we had rather inherited it to some extent in the course of our national movement for freedom. . . .

[3] From "Policy of Non-alignment Serves Cause of World Peace," report of speech by Prime Minister Nehru in Indian Parliament, March 17, 1959. *India News.* 4:3. Ap. 1, '59.

It is not a question of "purer than thou" attitude or high morality. We know our faults very well, and we know the virtues of others, sometimes even those we criticize. But gradually in the course of the years people came to realize that we were not moralizing, but that we were follwing a certain policy in all good faith and that policy while being one deliberately of friendship to other countries was yet one not only of nonalignment as such but something deeper than that, of doing something that we thought right in the circumstances.

Honorable members sometimes accuse us . . . about our complacence in regard to the U.S.-Pakistan Pact, that we have toned down our opposition to these things, and broadly hinted that this might be due to our desire to get American dollars for our development and not to say or do anything which might perhaps come in the way of that. Well, we have not been ashamed to get help from the United States or from the Soviet Union, and we propose to get that help from any country which gives aid on fair terms and expressly on terms that have nothing to do with our policy. I am really grieved at this idea being put out, that our policy is governed by the lure of dollars or whatever it may be. We are liable to error, but one thing I think might be taken for granted. That is, where the honor and interests of India are concerned we are not going to give in, whatever the consequences may be, not only in terms of financial help, even other consequences.

In the old days when in the United Nations or elsewhere, we adopted an attitude in support of some proposition, if that proposition was, let us say, supported also by the Soviet group, then it was suggested "These people under the cover of their nonalignment and so-called neutrality are secretly assisting the Soviet group." If we voted for the other group led by the United States, then it was said "There you are, in search of dollars; they are doing this in search of something else."

People did not seem to realize that a country can act just on the merits of a question and not under pressures and fears. I do believe that in spite of our numerous problems and numerous difficulties, India is a country today in the wide world which is least afraid of other countries, whatever they may be.

Today there are many problems. Yet from the world point of view the biggest problem, judged from the point of view of war or peace, is still the problem of Berlin in Germany. I am not going into that. I have always avoided going into that because one cannot make oneself responsible for the big problems of the world. Naturally because it is an important problem we have given thought to it; we have discussed it with other people; we have in our own way made some minor suggestions as to what should be done. But all those, even the suggestions, that we have made, are also not on what policies should be pursued, but that any policy should be pursued with a measure of gentleness and not abuse. That, I submit, is a slightly distinctive feature of India. Not from today, but certainly from Buddha and Asoka's time and right down to Gandhi's time, and it makes all the difference how you do a thing. If you do a right thing with abuse, that right thing becomes a wrong thing and it does not lead to results, while even a wrong thing may become a right thing if it is done gently and in a friendly way.

It (Berlin) is a very big problem, a tremendous problem. On that depends the future of war or peace—maybe this very year, maybe in six months, or three months' time. What is the good of my sitting down and according to my thinking logically condemning this person or that nation?

I am glad to learn . . . that President Eisenhower has accepted the idea of having a summit conference; that is, to say, he has suggested, I believe, first of all that a meeting of Foreign Ministers might take place and later a summit conference . . . in the next two or three months. So I do think that the pressure of events and the general feeling among people in all countries is driving governments and leaders of countries towards this approach of consultation. . . .

U.S.-Pakistan Defense Pact

I start by saying that we do not think condemnation is the right approach. I do believe that the United States of America has the friendliest feelings for us, by and large. It may be that its policies moved by other considerations push it in other

directions; that is a different matter: just as I do believe that the
Soviet Union has the friendliest feelings for us. It is a matter
of great satisfaction to us that we can follow a policy, a policy
which I say is a straightforward policy which yet gets to us
friendly feelings from great and small countries which are hostile
and antagonistic to each other. And this is not due to any
cleverness on our part or any wonderful feat of policy. It is
due basically, as I said, right at the beginning, to that little touch
—a very little touch, I am sorry to say, but still a touch—of the
Gandhian in us that still functions. Therefore, there can be no
doubt that from the point of view of any pact, these military
alliance pacts, we disapprove of them. We think they do not
bring security; they bring insecurity.

So far as this particular matter is concerned, this bilateral pact,
naturally we have other considerations also because it affects
India. It affects India even though the United States government
does not want it to affect India. I believe honestly, I believe that
they do not want it to affect India for other reasons. But though
they do not want it to affect India, it does affect India. It is a
facts that it does affect India, because in the nature of things
such a development has to affect India because of Indo-Pakistan
relations, because of Pakistan being our neighbor.

THE KASHMIR PROBLEM [4]

The Kashmir case has been dogging the United Nations for
so long, the debates have been so wearisome, the arguments so
repetitious, that it is easy to assume that nothing has really
changed, that it is all unimportant, and that the same old record
simply keeps spinning on the political turntable.

This is quite easy—and quite wrong. The fact is that in the
past nine years the case of Kashmir has built up a set of attitudes
and habits of thinking in India and Pakistan which have an
importance far transcending the boundaries of the two countries.
For these attitudes and ways of thinking color the way Indians
and Pakistanis see the rest of the world.

[4] From "Kashmir's Far-reaching Impact," by A. M. Rosenthal, correspondent of
the New York *Times*. *Foreign Policy Bulletin*. 36:93-5. Mr. 1, '57. Reprinted by
permission.

In the West there is a natural tendency to think about
Pakistani or Indian foreign policy strictly in terms of the West's
own problems. The United States feels a natural warmth toward
Pakistan because since September 8, 1954, that country has
become part of our military structure. By contrast, there is a
coldness toward India because, at best, India stands aloof and
often shows a determined understanding of the problems and
fears of Russia and Communist China which it cannot seem to
muster for the West.

But to a degree that is difficult to exaggerate, the foreign
policy of Pakistan and India is based, not on great problems of
global strategy, but on each other and most especially on Kashmir.

This reporter, for instance, has yet to meet a Pakistani who
in frank conversation would argue seriously that his country
entered the Western military alliance because of fear of attack by
Russia or China. Pakistan wants arms, not against the Communist
nations, but against India. This does not mean that the Pakistanis
are arming for a swift, knockout attack against India. It does
mean that the Pakistanis think they can only be in a position to
deal with India diplomatically and politically if they are militarily
strong.

Kashmir Colors Policies

As for the Indians, it is Pakistan, more than the United States
or the Soviet Union, which determines how they will act or
react. The Indians say they are against military pacts, but they
have little to say about any pacts except those which involve
Pakistan. The United States has told New Delhi that arms given
to Pakistan will never be used against India. But it is more than
a little naïve of Americans to expect Indians to base the security
of their country on this promise.

And it is Pakistan and Kashmir which determine to an important extent how Indians react to the Soviet Union. An Indian
editor once told this reporter that he simply could not understand
why Americans were puzzled about India's warmth or at least
caution toward Moscow. To him things were fairly simple.
The possibility existed that India and Pakistan would one day
get into a war over Kashmir. When that day came, India would

want to have friends, good friends, in the United Nations Security Council. It would want friends who would give it material help.

The influence of Kashmir goes beyond the attitudes of India and Pakistan toward the major powers. It also determines how both countries react to the smaller nations.

For several years now, India has been carrying on an intensive and quite successful campaign to make friends with the Moslem nations. The gains have been obvious. King Saud of Saudi Arabia and . . . [the former president] of Syria both have given "good chits" to India—statements that India treats its Moslem population of over 40 million well. This has caused pain and anger in Pakistan. But more important is the fact that the Indians have dashed Pakistani hopes of uniting the Moslem world against India's occupation of Kashmir. Pakistani newspapermen and officials try hard to get visiting Moslem statesmen to commit themselves on this—and usually fail.

Indians, of course, pay a political price for this, but it is not terribly heavy. It has mostly to do with consistency and morality, and New Delhi seems to be willing to pay this price. Just about every time nations have found themselves in a dispute which brought them to the brink of war or over it, India has used all its influence to get a peace settlement or at least get direct negotiations going. This has been the case in Indo-China and in Korea. It has been the case in the dispute between Washington and Peiping, between Moscow and Washington. "Negotiate, negotiate," the Indians have always said. But not when it comes to the Arab-Israeli controversy. Nehru obviously has some weight and influence in the Arab world—but he has refused to use them in favor of Arab-Israeli talks. The reason, quite obviously, is that he would run the danger of antagonizing the Moslem nations he has been cultivating so carefully for so long.

The Pakistanis, too, see the Moslem nations they once counted as brothers through the spectacles of Kashmir. . . .

Thus India and Pakistan seem to have arrived at one fundamental agreement about Kashmir. Both countries use it as a yardstick judging other nations and for shaping their own policies. It is not the only Indian or Pakistani yardstick, but it is the most important one.

Kashmir and Internal Affairs

The story of Kashmir has also had important psychological and political effects within India and Pakistan.

In Pakistan, the case of Kashmir has been simultaneously a source of national frustration and of political escapism. So long as the Moslem majority of Kashmir is denied a chance to express its opinion by plebiscite, no Pakistani government can feel it is a successful government. This sense of almost unbearable frustration becomes even stronger the farther one travels in West Pakistan from Karachi. In Azad Kashmir, the area held by Pakistan, government officials say there is only one way to get what they feel religiously and emotionally is theirs by right, and that is the way of war. There is bitterness against India, naturally; but there is also bitterness against Karachi for standing in the way of war, and bitterness against the United States and Britain for not coming fully to the aid of an ally.

This frustration has been a burden for Pakistan. But some Pakistani politicians have found it convenient to be able to blame India, the West, the East—just about everybody but themselves— for their country's economic, political and diplomatic troubles. . . .

In India the Kashmir case has contributed to the already rather fully developed national myopia.

It came as something of a shock to Indians to find that the Security Council would vote 10 to 0 in favor of a resolution which in effect declared the accession of Kashmir to India illegal without a plebiscite. This should not have been a shock. For years it has been clear that most of the world considered India wrong in its refusal to allow a plebiscite, no matter how urgent and real its reasons may be. And since even some Indians are beginning to realize that V. K. Krishna Menon, the latest man to take over the job of presenting India's case, is a spectacular failure at winning friends for his country, there was no reason to expect a change. . . .

With the shock came rationalizations, another side-effect of the Kashmir case. "The world would not listen to India's case." "The Council's judgment was based on power politics, not legalities or moralities." "Our friends deserted us." "People are against us." "Earlier Indian delegates did a terrible job." All sorts of reasons have been advanced, except the obvious one that whether India is right or wrong in Kashmir, it has not been able to convince the world that it is right.

This refusal to see can be carried to almost incredible lengths. India makes it clear it will not abide by a United Nations decision, yet a few days later Mr. Krishna Menon berates Israel for not carrying out a United Nations decision. And nobody in India seems to think: Is this not a little strange?

India's Kashmir Achievements

There is another place where the Kashmir case has produced reactions and results which do not show up in United Nations debates or resolutions—and that is Kashmir.

Economically, the Indians are doing a good job in their part of Kashmir, in some ways a better job than is being done in some parts of India. Schools are built, villagers are taught improved methods of agriculture, rice is made cheap, irrigation canals are dug, a powerhouse and year-round tunnel are constructed. Land reform is carried through ruthlessly. The big landowners may object, but the peasants do not. Farmers get credits, and craftsmen and shopkeepers get tourists.

Politically, India and Bakshi Ghulam Mohammed, Moslem prime minister of the Indian-held part of Kashmir, have established an authoritarian state. The normal place of residence for opposition leaders is jail. Indian leaders are embarrassed by this, know it is a blot on India's political record, and talk of relaxing their control, but so far it is just talk.

Pakistanis say that economic benefits will not win over Kashmir's Moslems, that India is a colonial power, and that history has shown that colonialists cannot "buy" the people under them. This is a bit too pat. India may not be the country Kashmiris would choose, given a free choice, but neither is it a foreign colonial power. . . .

The Indians believe that time is on their side. The more frank among them admit that a plebiscite would favor Pakistan. But they think that year by year the Pakistani majority is being whittled down and that one day—ten years, say, or twenty years from now—it may all be academic.

The Pakistanis hope and believe that in their optimism the Indians are making a big mistake. And certainly the record of the Kashmir case has been one of mistakes committed by both sides, mistakes from the purely pragmatic, or winner-take-all, point of view.

The greatest mistake was a military one made by Pakistan. In 1947, when the Kashmir conflict started, the Moslem tribesmen, after crossing Pakistani territory and fighting in Kashmir under Pakistani officers, had just about achieved victory. They were at a place called Baramula, about thirty miles from the valley's only airport at Srinagar. The tribesmen stopped for a bit of looting and raping at Baramula, and by the time they had had enough the Indians had taken over the airport and begun that remarkable airlift from New Delhi which was to give India the Vale of Kashmir.

India's errors were political, although not quite as expensive as those of Pakistan because it was in occupation. . . .

Mistakes by India led to the greatest mistake of all—the failure to put across to the rest of the world what to India has become the essence of the Kashmir case. Once wrapped up in promises that would not be heeded, in reports that would not be implemented, India found itself unable to hammer home the one basic point.

Bireligious Survival

That point is that as far as India is concerned, the case of Kashmir involves not just the future of a valley but the future of a nation. No responsible Indian leader would be willing to forecast that the bireligious basis of this country would not be destroyed if Moslem Kashmir "deserted" India and went to Pakistan.

Perhaps "bireligious" is too strong a word. But there are 40 million Moslems in India, living among eight times as many Hindus. They live in an uneasy peace, a peace which could be shattered by something far less dramatic than evidence through a plebiscite that every Moslem in India would prefer to be a

Moslem in Pakistan. Indian officials are afraid that an orgy of bloodletting would sweep India after a plebiscite in favor of Pakistan. They may be wrong, but as people who are in command and must accept the responsibility of government, they are not taking the chance.

To all this the Pakistanis say, "religious blackmail." They say this is proof that the Moslems in India are hostages. They say this is proof that the Indian government cannot control its own country.

All these charges have some truth in them. But true or not, they do not alter the basic fact that no Indian government can afford to take a risk which conceivably—not certainly, but at least conceivably—could destroy the nation.

NEHRU ON TIBET [5]

In the course of the last few days, reports have reached us that a considerable number of Tibetans numbering some thousands have recently crossed into Kameng frontier division of the North East Frontier Agency and some hundreds have also entered territory of Bhutan.

They sought asylum and we have agreed to this. Such of them as carried arms were disarmed.

Temporary arrangements are being made in a camp for their maintenance until they can be dispersed in accordance with their wishes and necessities governing such cases. . . .

A tragedy has been and is being enacted in Tibet. Passions have been let loose, charges made and language used which cannot but worsen the situation and our relations with our northern neighbor.

I am sure that the House will agree with me that in considering matters of such high import, we should exercise restraint and wisdom and use language which is moderate and precise. In these days of the cold war there has been a tendency to use unrestrained language and often to make wild charges without any justification.

[5] From "Excerpts from Nehru's Statement [in the Indian Parliament] on Situation in Tibet," as reprinted in New York *Times*. New York *Times*. p 12. Ap. 28, '59.

We have fortunately kept out of the cold war and I hope that on this, as on any other occasion, we shall not use the language of the cold war.

The matter is too serious to be dealt with in a trivial or excited way. I would therefore appeal to the press and public to exercise restraint in language. . . .

In the excitement of the moment we cannot allow ourselves to be swept away into wrong courses.

It is not for me to make any similar appeal to the leaders, press, and people of China. All I can say is that I have been greatly distressed at the tone of the comments and charges made against India by responsible people in China.

They have used the language of the cold war regardless of truth and propriety. This is peculiarly distressing in a great nation with thousands of years of culture behind it, noted for its restrained and polite behavior.

The charges made against India are so fantastic that I find it difficult to deal with them. . . .

[An] allegation has been made about "Indian expansionists" who, it is alleged, are inheritors of the British tradition of imperialism and expansion.

It is perfectly true that British policy was one of expansion into Tibet and that they carried this out by force of arms early in this century.

That was, in our opinion, an unjustified and cruel adventure which brought much harm to the Tibetans.

As a result of that, the then British government in India established certain extraterritorial rights in Tibet. When India became independent, we inherited some of these rights.

Being entirely opposed to any such extraterritorial rights in another country, we did not wish to retain them. But in the early days after independence and partition, our hands were full, as this House well knows, and we had to face very difficult situations in our country.

Soon after Chinese armies entered Tibet the question of these extraterritorial rights was raised and we readily agreed to give them up.

We would have given them up anyhow, whatever developments might have taken place in Tibet.

We withdrew our army detachments from some places in Tibet and handed over Indian postal and telegraph installations and rest houses.

Our action in this matter and whatever we have done subsequently in regard to Tibet is proof enough of our policy and that India had no political or ulterior ambitions in Tibet.

Ever since then we have endeavored not only to act up to the agreement we made but to cultivate the friendship of the Chinese state and people.

It is therefore a matter of the deepest regret and surprise to us that charges should be made which are both unbecoming and entirely void of substance. . . .

I stated some time ago that our broad policy was governed by three factors—preservation of the security and integrity of India, our desire to maintain friendly relations with China, and our deep sympathy for the people of Tibet.

That policy we shall continue to follow because we think that a correct policy not only for the present but even more so for the future.

We for our part will follow this policy but we hope that China also will do likewise and that nothing will be said or done which endangers the friendly relations of two countries which are so important from the wider point of view of the peace of Asia and the world. . . .

When Premier Chou En-lai came here two or three years ago he was good enough to discuss Tibet with me at considerable length. He told me that while Tibet had long been a part of the Chinese state, they did not consider Tibet as a province of China.

Therefore, they considered Tibet an autonomous region which would enjoy autonomy. He told me further that it was absurd for anyone to imagine that China was going to force communism on Tibet.

Meanwhile, change in some forms inevitably came to Tibet. Though physical barriers were progressively removed, mental and emotional barriers increased.

Apparently an attempt to cross these mental and emotional barriers was either not made or did not succeed.

To say that a number of "upper strata reactionaries" in Tibet were solely responsible for this, appears to be an extraordinary simplification of a complicated situation. Even according to accounts received through Chinese sources, the revolt in Tibet was of considerable magnitude and the basis of it must have been a strong feeling of nationalism which affects not only upper-class people but others also.

No doubt vested interests joined it and sought to profit by it. An attempt to explain the situation by the use of rather worn-out words, phrases and slogans is seldom helpful.

We have no desire whatever to interfere in Tibet. We have every desire to maintain friendship between India and China. But at the same time, we have every sympathy for the people of Tibet and we are greatly distressed at their hapless plight.

We hope still that the authorities of China in their wisdom will not use their great strength against the Tibetans but will win them to friendly cooperation in accordance with the assurances they have themselves given about the autonomy of the Tibet region. Above all, we hope that the present fighting and killing will cease.

INDIA UNDER PRESSURE [6]

Jawaharlal Nehru, leader of India since it became independent twelve years ago, is getting his lesson the hard way.

The Nehru government is in crisis. An angry Indian parliament has learned that Red Chinese troops have killed Indian soldiers inside India, have seized bits of Indian territory, have threatened to seize little countries under India's protection.

What is more, Mr. Nehru has finally been brought to face the fact that the Soviet Union—through Afghanistan—and Red China—through a "sneak war" in Laos—are trying to outflank India's military defenses.

The lesson now thrust upon Mr. Nehru is that his policy of "neutrality" is not working. All his best efforts to make friends

[6] From "Nehru Learns About Reds . . . the Hard Way." *U.S. News & World Report.* 47:35-8. S. 14, '59. Reprinted from *U.S. News & World Report,* an independent weekly news magazine published at Washington. Copyright 1959 United States News Publishing Corporation.

with the Communists of Mao Tse-tung's Red China and of
Khrushchev's Soviet Russia have failed to protect India itself,
have opened the way in South Asia for Red conquest.

The Indian Prime Minister, his friends are reporting, has not
abandoned his hope of checking Communist aggression with
words and negotiations. But he is, they insist, at last aware of
the tactics of the two great Communist powers, Red China and
Soviet Russia, now seeking to engulf all of South Asia.

The events of recent weeks are forcing Nehru to take a new
position of firmness toward Red aggression.

On August 25, some 200 to 300 Red Chinese troops, attacking from Tibet, overwhelmed a garrison of 67 Indian soldiers
within India in a two-day battle, killing several Indians, wound-
ing some, capturing others. The battle took place on the
frontier of northeast India.

At the end of August, Mr. Nehru faced an aroused Indian
parliament. In answer to questions from deputies, the Prime
Minister confirmed the August 25 attack. He told the deputies
of four previous skirmishes on the same frontier. He gave an
account of Red Chinese aggression against India dating back over
two years. Mr. Nehru also confirmed reports, current for months,
that the Chinese Reds had threatened India's two mountain
protectorates of Bhutan and Sikkim. The deputies were shocked,
angry, critical.

"There is no alternative but to defend our frontiers," the
Prime Minister told parliament. He added: "Any aggression
against Bhutan and Sikkim will be considered an aggression
against India."

This was strong talk for Mr. Nehru. For many years, in the
United Nations and elsewhere, the Indian Prime Minister has
appeared as a champion of negotiations with Red China, as a
critic of all anti-Communist alliances.

To back up such talk, Mr. Nehru ordered the Indian Army
to send strong forces of troops, trained for mountain and jungle
warfare, up to India's frontiers with Tibet. But Nehru ordered
Indian troops to carry out "a peaceful reoccupation"—without
firing a shot—of areas of India held by Chinese Reds.

There were more shocks for Mr. Nehru still to come.

On September 1, General Mohammed Ayub Khan, the
military leader who now is President of Pakistan, flew to New
Delhi. Mr. Nehru met him at the airport, where they talked for
an hour. General Ayub warned the Indian leader that Afghanistan is falling rapidly under Soviet domination, thus opening
the frontiers of Pakistan and of India to a Soviet attack
outflanking India on the West. . . .

On the East, Communist Chinese and their allies, if they take
Laos, will stand on the borders of Cambodia and Thailand, on
the eastern frontier of Burma, long considered vital to India's
defenses. In Laos, Communists are in a position to sweep into
all that is left of Southeast Asia's non-Communist countries—
South Vietnam, Thailand, Cambodia, Malaya, Burma, too. And,
in Burma, there is a heavy and steady infiltration of Chinese
"civilian" settlers from the north. From Burma's border mountains, Communists could strike into the densely populated valleys
of the Brahmaputra and Ganges rivers, leading to Calcutta, where
Indian Communists now are leading revolutionary riots.

On the West, the Soviet penetration of Afghanistan, according to U.S. observers, has reached dangerous proportions. Half
the country's foreign trade is in Soviet hands. Afghanistan's
army, equipped with Soviet weapons, is trained by a Soviet
military mission; Afghanistan's air force has 60 jet fighters and
12 jet bombers. Russian pilots are reported to be flying these
bombers in reconnaissance flights over Pakistan and India.

Particularly alarming to Pakistan's leaders and Indian military
men is the fact that Soviet engineers and technicians now are
engaged in a "crash" program to build a 475-mile highway. This
road leads from the Soviet railhead on Afghanistan's northern
border across the country to Kandahar. At Kandahar, it is to
connect with a U.S.-built highway leading to a railhead on
Pakistan's frontier, south of the Himalayas. Using this route, in
a war, Soviet forces could strike directly into the Indus River
valley, within easy reach of Bombay, India's largest city.

This grim strategic picture has long been a matter of concern
to Western military observers, to Pakistan, to many Indian
military leaders. But it is coming as a shock to many Indians.

Mr. Nehru, once considered "above criticism" in India, now is coming under heavy fire at home. . . .

It was in 1950 that the Chinese Communists first invaded Tibet. Early this year, after Chinese Reds had crushed revolt in Tibet, Pakistan's General Ayub proposed a common India-Pakistan defense organization. Mr. Nehru is reported to have replied: "Defense against whom?"

Now, as the Communist pincers are tightening on India, Mr. Nehru's followers are saying the Indian Prime Minister has learned his lesson. But critics, now more numerous, fear that the lesson may have been learned too late.

THE TIBETAN DEBATE [7]

India is doubtless going through an agonizing reappraisal of the nature of Chinese imperialism, but strikingly the Indian government seems determined to ignore any instance of Chinese expansionism that does not affect its own boundaries. This is, I know, a harsh judgment. But how else shall we explain the curious vote of the Indian delegate—or rather, his refusal to take part in any vote—on the question of debating the Tibetan issue in the UN?

If anyone in the United States thinks that Krishna Menon, through his position at the UN, is expressing the feeling of the Indian people, I can say flatly that he is wrong. This is one issue on which all parties and wings except the Communists are agreed, from the new Swatantra party to the Praja Socialist party. Tibet was the victim of a coldblooded shooting war by China, India is faced with a cynical penetration of her boundaries and erosion of her territory. But there is no mistaking the fact that the source is the same in each case and the source is Chinese imperialist expansionism.

Judging from the universal press condemnation of the Krishna Menon position at the UN, the Indian people are ashamed of it. Yet one should add that the policy is not Menon's alone. It is also Nehru's. The latter has recently been carrying on a speech campaign against the press as being

[7] From article by Max Lerner, historian and columnist. New York *Post*. p 48. O. 21, '59. Reprinted by permission.

part of the "private sector" of the economy, and therefore presumably putting profits ahead of truth. But on the Tibet issue the leading writers in the newspapers are closer to the truth, to the mood of the people, and to the moral position that India has claimed in the world than is Krishna Menon as Nehru's spokesman.

The public explanations of the Indian position are pretty feeble. The argument that China has not signed any Declaration of Human Rights and is not a member of the UN seems too cynical even for a latter-day Machiavellian. This would mean that the UN as a body must ignore even the cruelest acts of governments which for some reason have not signed a legal convention or are not members of the world body. It would make a nullity out of the entire role of the UN in the formation and strengthening of the moral opinion of mankind.

Nor can we take seriously the Indian position that a UN discussion of the Tibetan issue "will not help the Tibetan people." If Menon means that it will not bring dead Tibetans to life, nor revive the slaughtered corpse of Tibetan religion and culture, he is uttering the cruelest truism. By that logic no massacre should ever be discussed after it has taken place, and no question of the violation of human rights should ever be debated. This would mean silence about the South African treatment of the Indian minority there, and silence also on the Algerian question—both of them issues on which the Indian delegates are rather verbal. It also means that nothing should ever have been said about the Hungarian massacre, once the victims were dead.

There remains the argument that India must not allow itself to be dragged into the cold war, a position which is an outgrowth of the basic Indian policy of nonalignment with either camp. It is difficult to see how an earnest and honest attempt to inquire into what happened to the Tibetan people and culture will increase the cold war. To be sure, the Chinese will not like it, but if that is to be the test then the Nehru position would rule out anything that ruffles the feelings of the Russians and Chinese. These are not the outlines of a policy: they are the blueprints of a moral abdication.

The truth is that while there has been a new revolution in Asian opinion, which now is beginning to see the visage of Chinese imperialism, this revolution has not yet reshaped Indian foreign policy itself—as it is bound in the end to reshape it.

In a stern note two weeks ago to Chou En-lai, Nehru said that India would never submit to having its boundaries changed by force. He said he was willing to negotiate about what had happened thus far, but that any further incursions would be resisted. . . .

The importance of the Indian refusal to vote on the Tibetan revolution is that it shows up the contradictions in India's whole position. By trying to keep the Tibetan issue quiet, and by refusing to speak out against Chinese designs against Laos, the Indian government is saying to the Chinese: "Settle your quarrel with us. We have no quarrel with you about what you are doing to others."

A great moral leader of Indian opinion like Jayaprakash Nalayan is deeply troubled about this. So is the Praja Socialist Party, under the leadership of Asoka Mehta. They have reason to be troubled. For by refusing to see the situation of others as comparable to their own, the Indian government leaders are allowing their own moral position in the world to be eroded.

They talk privately of their national security as the crucial guide of their policy, and point out that they are caught between Chinese and Russian power on their boundaries. But their national security lies, in part at least, in their moral position in world opinion. They cannot afford to throw it away in the interests of a power politics game which can be played by a nation with vast military and economic power far better than it can be played by India.

WHAT DOES CHINA WANT? [8]

The Chinese Communists have now made their comment on the sad little Tibetan debate in the UN—by all but wiping

[8] From "Really Hog-Wild?" by Joseph Alsop, newspaper columnist and author. New York *Herald Tribune.* p 18. O. 26, '59. © 1959, New York *Herald Tribune Inc.* Reprinted by permission.

out a troop of Indian soldiers on the disputed Indian-Tibetan border.

To a great many people, this new brand of Chinese Communist aggression is not merely alarming. It is also totally bewildering. Jawaharlal Nehru himself recently told a visitor that not so long ago "Chou En-lai absolutely sat at my feet," seeking instruction "as a pupil might seek guidance" from a revered teacher. What on earth, Nehru sadly asked, had caused the terrible change in Chou and his government?

There are analyists here, however, who do not look at the Chinese Communists with Nehru's blinkers. These able men offer a perfectly coherent explanation of the border episodes, which is well worth summarizing.

On the one hand, the hopes that the Chinese Communists cherished when Chou En-lai used to sit at Nehru's feet have now been severely disappointed. Sweetness and light . . . have not paid off in the tangible form of important gains by the Asian Communist parties. After long hesitation, Nehru himself liquidated the biggest gain that had been achieved, by suspending the Communist government of the Indian state of Kerala.

On the other hand, Peiping could not continue the policy of sweetness and light, while suppressing the Tibetan rebellion with the necessary ferocity. When they were forced to choose between good public relations in Asia and firm control of Tibet, the Chinese Communists did not hesitate for an instant. "What we have we hold," is their motto.

The Tibetan rebellion, in turn, created the necessity for the border incidents. The two Chinese Communist viceroys there, Generals Chang Kuo-hua and Chang Ching-wu, have not crushed the dissidents despite their utter ruthlessness. They have only five Chinese divisions in Tibet. Yet the task of supplying these troops in active operations, across the trackless, fuel-less, food-less roof of the world, is a heavy burden for overstrained China. The pressure to get the job finished must therefore be great.

Hope is the great nourisher of all rebellions. With the Dalai Lama a refugee in India, the need was surely felt to show the Tibetan dissidents that India offered them no hope. What could be more useful, then, than troop movements on the border, to assert the territorial claims long made by Peiping, and also to show that the Indians are weak and easily bullied?

Such is the remarkably convincing expert explanation of this ugly business. It leaves only one area of mystery, the area of the relations between Communist China and Soviet Russia. For it is pretty certain that Peiping's shows of force on the Indian border have not been approved by Moscow. Does this mean, then, that Nikita S. Khrushchev "can no longer restrain" Mao Tse-tung, as some people say? Is Mao now really going hog-wild?

The best tentative answer to these questions lies in the nature of the border incidents. They are military operations, but they do not involve the slightest military risk for China. At times in the past, when under special stress, the Chinese have ventured to take action on their own hook—as long as no military risk was involved. The most important instance of this character was the Indian proposal for a Korean truce, which so enraged Joseph Stalin. The proposal actually emanated from Chou En-lai, via the Indian Ambassador in Peiping; and this was why Stalin was so angry.

But at no time in the past have the Chinese Communists ever taken any action involving any military risk, without securing Moscow's prior approval. Last year's probe at Quemoy, concerted at the Peiping meeting of Mao, Khrushchev and their defense ministers, is the classic case in point. All the other past cases fit the same pattern. It is still reasonable to expect that the pattern will hold.

It is also reasonable to expect, however, that the Sino-Soviet partnership will go on puzzling simple people by the seeming conflict between the peaceable Khrushchev and the warlike Mao. In any partnership, after all, it is extremely useful for one partner to show the world a smiling, friendly face, while the other partner plays the hard-nosed role. The outer contrast need not imply inner disagreement.

EFFECTS OF CHINESE PRESSURE ON
INDIA-PAKISTAN RELATIONS [9]

Communist China is entitled to much of the credit for the progress being made by India and Pakistan in disposing of the common problems that remained to be settled after they achieved independence. A provisional agreement has now been reached on most of the frontier between India and West Pakistan, and this is only the latest sign of the desire of the two countries to improve their relations. . . .

However, bad feeling between India and Pakistan now has such a long history that a dramatic improvement is unlikely, unless Communist China should emerge as an immediate and unmistakable danger to both countries.

Field Marshal Ayub, the President of Pakistan, took the initiative . . . [in September 1959], when he issued a statement at the New Delhi airport calling for a rational approach to the problems facing India and his country in a spirit of good neighborliness.

Such words had not been heard on the Indian subcontinent since August 1947 when Britain, over the strong opposition of the Hindu Congress party, coupled the grant of independence with the establishment of Pakistan as a Moslem state.

Prime Minister Nehru's response has not been as cordial; but clearly there is a strong movement in both countries in favor of terminating the unfriendliness in relations that has prevailed since the partition of the subcontinent.

The heritage of bad feeling began when hundreds of thousands of persons were killed in the religious riots that followed the grant of independence. The resulting ill will did not have a chance to die down before India and Pakistan became engaged in a dispute over Kashmir, where the Hindu Maharaja had placed his subjects under Indian rule despite the fact that the majority of the Kashmiri are Moslems.

[9] From "Peiping Action Spurs India-Pakistan Amity," by Thomas J. Hamilton, New York *Times* correspondent. New York *Times*. p E3. Ja. 17, '60. Reprinted by permission.

Moslem tribesmen from the Northwest Frontier, later joined
by units of the Pakistani Army, rushed in on one side of Kashmir
and Indian troops on the other.

A full scale war was avoided through action by the United
Nations Security Council, which obtained a cease-fire New Year's
Day, 1949. However, the Security Council never succeeded in
inducing the two governments to accept arrangements for a
plebiscite to determine the status of Kashmir.

Relations between the Indian and Pakistani governments were
further embittered when Pakistan, having become a party to the
Southeast Asia Defense Treaty in September 1954, began receiving large quantities of United States military equipment.

Indians charged that this was more likely to be used against
India than against Communist China or the Soviet Union. This
suspicion was, in fact, partly responsible for the policy of neutrality Mr. Nehru adopted in the "cold war."

Mr. Nehru's criticism of the United States became less fre-
quent after the Soviet Union's savage repression of the revolt in
Hungary in 1956 and the stand taken by the United States
against Britain, France and Israel in the Suez crisis at that time.

It would seem that Communist China's actions in the last
year, together with President Ayub's stand in favor of a settlement, prompted both India and Pakistan to modify their insistence
upon positions that had blocked progress for a decade.

Since September [1959] there have been considerable ad-
vances in three areas:

(1) *Financial problems.* These arose out of the partition
settlement, notably the apportionment of the national debt and
the valuation to be put on each country's share of the railroads,
post and telegraph facilities which had served the subcontinent
under British rule. Financial experts of India and Pakistan have
made such progress in recent negotiations that their finance
ministers are expected to reach an over-all agreement in February
[1960].

(2) *Demarcation of the frontier.* Virtually complete agreement on the frontiers between India and East Pakistan was
reached last fall. Only one section of the India-West Pakistan

frontier was omitted from the provisional agreement. The atmosphere is hopeful, and it is expected that the rectifications of the frontier, which will involve exchanging a number of villages, will take place in October [1960].

(3) *Allocation of the water of the Indus River System.* The rivers rise in India and the Indian-held part of Kashmir; the waters are needed to supply irrigation canals in Pakistan. The negotiations, which have been under way in Washington since 1954 under the auspices of the International Bank for Reconstruction and Development, have made progress in recent months. If all continues to go well, it is believed that a water-use treaty will be signed in March [1960].

An Indus River settlement would be of much value in reducing tension over Kashmir. Most of Kashmir's practical importance derives from the fact that political control carries with it control over the headwaters of the Indus and other great rivers that flow through both countries. If India and Pakistan agree on water rights, friction over Kashmir will be less important.

However, the national prestige of both India and Pakistan is now committed; and for the time being it is impossible for either government to agree publicly to what appears to be the only possible solution—partition.

India has revoked her original acceptance of a plebiscite and holds that the Maharaja's decision in 1947 assigned all of Kashmir to India for all time. For good measure, Kashmiri representatives have sat in the Indian Parliament since 1954.

The cease-fire line, therefore, is now the dividing line for an area the size of Kansas. Three million Kashmiri are under Indian rule and the other one million are citizens of Azad Kashmir (Free Kashmir), which is nominally autonomous but actually controlled by Pakistan.

This *de facto* partition seems likely to become permanent. If India and Pakistan, without making public statements, simply acquiesce in the continuance of partition, they could leave the issue to be settled later in the better atmosphere foreshadowed by current negotiations.

IV. INDIA AND AMERICA

EDITOR'S INTRODUCTION

What should be the policy of the United States toward India? Many experts believe this has been a crucial issue in American foreign policy from the end of World War II. It is not one that has been given top priority, but may well receive it in the very near future should India's problems at home or abroad deteriorate into acute crisis.

Currently U.S.-Indian relations are warmer than at any time since the war. This was symbolized by the extraordinary welcome accorded President Eisenhower on his short trip to India last December. That trip was not a time for negotiations regarding increased assistance for India. But both Indian and American spokesmen indicate that India's needs will receive renewed emphasis during the coming year.

Possible military conflict with Red China aside, it has become increasingly clear that India does face a crisis at home within a few years. As noted in Section II above, its economic development has been retrenched, but the pressures on its resources from an expanding population have not relented. Most authorities agree that further outside aid for India is necessary. This section deals mainly with American attitudes and policies with regard to such possible further aid.

The first article sketches the short history of Indian-American relations and notes recent changes for the better. Views pro and con are then given on United States aid to India. First is a major address to the Senate by Senator John F. Kennedy, followed by a statement in support of the Senator's proposal and by an argument against aid. In pursuing its economic development program India has already received significant aid from both the Western countries and the Soviet Union. The extent of this aid is given in the statistics which comprise the next selection. Following this is an interesting suggestion which may be made by Indian officials on how American surplus agricultural commodities might be used to stabilize India's food supply.

Averell Harriman, who traveled in India last year before the Tibetan revolt, summarizes his views on the current direction which Indian foreign policy is taking. Then Walter Lippmann exhorts us to support India's democracy lest India and with it most of Asia be lost by default to communism.

The final speeches by President Eisenhower are two which he gave in India last December, one before a vast throng near New Delhi and the other his radio farewell speech.

INDIA-UNITED STATES RELATIONS [1]

On January 3, 1959, a new American embassy was dedicated in the diplomatic enclave outside of New Delhi. Designed by Edward D. Stone, who also designed the American building at the Brussels International Exhibition, it is an impressive rectangular, windowless, two-story structure with marble lattice work, an inner wall of glass, a flat roof, and an extensive underground section.

Indian reactions to the new center of official American activities in India were as mixed as the reactions to United States foreign policy generally. Some regarded it as a great compliment that "the most pretentious embassy ever built by the United States" should be located in India, while others expressed the view that such magnificence was out of place in a land of hungry millions. Many commentators saw a symbolic significance in the location of the new embassy, between lots assigned to the Soviet Union and Communist China on a street whose name— Panch Shed Marg—is already being loosely translated as the street of peaceful coexistence. . . .

The dedication of a magnificent new American embassy in the capital of India is testimony to the importance of the relations between the two countries, and to their prominent roles

[1] From "India and the United States: Maturing Relations," by Norman D. Palmer, professor of political science, University of Pennsylvania. *Current History.* 36:129-34. Mr. '59. Reprinted by permission.

in world politics. For both the United States and India the postwar years have been eventful ones. The United States has become the most powerful nation of the non-Communist world, with growing commitments and responsibilities at a time when relations with the Soviet Union have become so tense as to raise doubts of the possibility of peaceful coexistence and when these unhappy relations are even more disturbing because of the startling developments in nuclear energy and destructive power.

India, after decades of foreign rule and nationalist agitation, has achieved independence, at the cost of partition, and has embarked on a fateful struggle to make that independence meaningful for the masses of its people in the face of internal difficulties and external pressures that place its future in jeopardy. Although it is now a weak nation, it plays a role in world affairs far out of relation to its actual power. It is the most populous of the non-Communist states, and the most important underdeveloped nation outside the Communist orbit. It is the leading spokesman of the "uncommitted world," and of the Asian-African group in the United Nations. Its policy of nonalignment, while much criticized in the United States, gives it a greater freedom of movement, flexibility of policy, and influence in international affairs than it would have if it were associated closely with any power constellation. . . .

In recent years the relations between the United States and India have been characterized by the usual ups and downs, with some evidences that these relations are maturing and that the two countries are beginning to understand each other better. Two developments in 1956 did a great deal to improve Indo-American relations. These were the opposition of the United States to the Anglo-French-Israeli invasion of Egypt and Nehru's visit to the United States in December. To be sure, the favorable climate created by these two developments was somewhat affected by certain almost simultaneous happenings; for example, Nehru was severely criticized in the United States—and in India as well—for his unwonted reticence regarding Russian brutalities in Hungary, and India was displeased by the vote of the United States on the Kashmir question in the Security Council of the

United Nations.   At a news conference in Washington on
December 19, 1956, Nehru said that the policy of the United
States toward "neutralist" nations like India "is not as rigid
as I thought," and was indeed "a flexible policy adapting itself
to circumstances."

Both countries have been well served by their ambassadors.
Chester Bowles made a profound impression upon Indians during his service as United States ambassador to India in 1951-
1953.   He was an effective interpreter of America in India,
and since his return to the United States he has been an equally
effective interpreter of India in his own country.   His successors,
George V. Allen, John Sherman Cooper and Ellsworth Bunker
have carried on in his tradition, and have also been cordially
received in India.

In 1958, G. L. Mehta concluded a long period of service
in the United States as Indian ambassador.   He had made hosts
of friends in the United States, and had been indefatigable in
his efforts to promote a better understanding of India and of
India's policies.   Unfortunately some months elapsed before
his successor, Mohammed C. Chagla, arrived in Washington
to assume his duties as ambassador.   Chagla is a former Chief
Justice of the High Court of Bombay and one of India's best-
known Moslems.   He should be able to represent India in the
high traditions that were established by Mr. Mehta and his
predecessors.

Sympathetic American reactions to India's needs for foreign
assistance in financing its second Five-Year Plan, the interest
shown in the visits to the United States of the Finance Ministers
of India, T. T. Krishnamachari in 1957 and Moraji Desai in
1958, and the granting of substantial loans to India in 1958
were welcomed appreciatively in India.

Conversely, Indians were far from sympathetic with three
major aspects of American policy in the summer of 1958.   The
dispatch of American troops to Lebanon was criticized as an
ill-advised venture in strong-arm diplomacy, with colonial over-
tones.   United States support of the resistance of the Chinese
Nationalists on Quemoy was regarded as another unfortunate

consequence of the shortsighted American policy regarding China, and as a dangerous gambit which increased international tensions. Worst of all in Indian eyes were the evidences of racial bigotry in the American South, of which the name Little Rock became the symbol. Indians are especially sensitive on issues of race and color, and the news from Little Rock required no Communist distortion to raise fresh doubts of the capacity of Americans to deal on terms of equality, justice and mutual respect with the colored peoples of the world.

Nuclear Test Ban

Indian opinion in both official and unofficial circles continues to be critical of the position of the United States regarding the testing of nuclear weapons and regarding the value of security pacts. India finds that it is inescapably affected by the tensions resulting from the cold war, a situation which, as Nehru remarked in the Lok Sabba (the Indian House of the People) on December 8, 1958, "covers every question in the world today." The spectacle of two giant powers, armed with atomic weapons, and eyeing each other malevolently, is certainly a frightening reality. Indians believe that it is a necessary step toward the reduction of international tensions to call a halt to the arms race, and particularly to stop the testing of nuclear weapons. . . .

The Pakistan Dispute

In . . . [an] important foreign policy address [on December 8, 1958] Nehru reaffirmed India's long-standing objections to security pacts, with particular reference to the two pacts which impinge most directly on India, namely the Southeast Asia Treaty and the Baghdad Pact. He pointed out that as a result of the establishment of military dictatorships in the areas presumably covered by these two pacts, and particularly in Pakistan and Iraq, the pacts had "no reality left" and were being kept alive solely for reasons of prestige. He also restated a basic Indian complaint against the United States when he declared that relations with Pakistan had been made more difficult by the "considerable military aid" which Pakistan was receiving from the United States. These relations, he believed, had become even more delicate since the suspension of parliamentary government and the establishment of military rule in Pakistan on October 7, 1958. . . .

Because of the delicate nature of the relations between India and Pakistan, American military assistance to Pakistan was always of dubious value, and in the light of recent developments in Pakistan it is likely to cause even more serious embarrassment to the United States as well as to India.

Tangible evidence of the deep interest of the United States in India's struggle to deal with its basic economic and social problems and to survive as a democratic state is afforded by the economic assistance which the United States has extended to free India. . . .

Second Five-Year Plan

The crisis in India's second Five-Year Plan, which was in effect a crisis in India's national existence, was generally appreciated in the United States, and was regarded as a challenge to the capacity and the willingness of the more prosperous democratic nations to assist the underdeveloped nations of the world to cope with their economic problems by democratic means. In 1958, the United States made two loans to India, of $75 million and $100 million respectively, out of the new Development Loan Fund, and the Export-Import Bank blazed new paths for its operations by extending a loan of $150 million for general categories of equipment and services. In June and in September representatives of India and the United States signed agreements for the sale to India of somewhat more than $300 million worth of United States surplus agricultural commodities under Public Law 480, with the provision that most of the Indian rupees accruing under the agreements would be used for loans to India for the financing of economic development projects.

In 1958, also, several concessions were made to India regarding the repayment of interest on previous loans. . . .

Trade with the United States

Trade between the United States and India is still relatively limited, and the amount of American private investment in India is very small. Generally speaking, American businessmen find it difficult to do business with underdeveloped countries which are dedicated to what Indian leaders call the "socialist pattern of society." For them the risks and restrictions are too great. In recent years, however, several developments have improved the prospects for American private investment in India and for mutual trade between the two countries. A major step was the signing in September, 1957, of an investment treaty. Negotiations for this treaty, the thirty-fifth to be signed under the United States investment guarantee program, had been initiated in April, 1955, and had encountered all kinds of obstacles and delays. Under this treaty the United States government will guarantee American private investors that their earnings from investments in India can be converted into dollars; it will not extend guarantees against nationalization or expropriation or the risks of war. . . .

The shared objectives of the United States and India form the bedrock on which good relations between the two countries, based on mutual friendship and respect, are founded. "Our two republics," said Nehru in a radio and television address to the American people on December 18, 1956, during his second visit to the United States, "share a common faith in democratic institutions and the democratic way of life, and are dedicated to the cause of peace and freedom."

What is important [he stated nearly a year later, in speaking to a group of American technical experts working in India] is the basic approach between one country and another. In regard to that I am quite convinced that the basic approach of India and the United States, in spite of often hard criticism on either side, is a friendly approach, is an appreciative approach, an approach with a desire to understand and improve relations between each other.

In spite of continued misunderstandings and criticisms Indians and Americans are beginning to know each other better and to appreciate each other's problems and aspirations. Fortunately this growing maturity of viewpoint is being reflected in the official relations of the two countries, and in their foreign policies generally.

THE ECONOMIC GAP [2]

Mr. President, the attention of the Congress and the American people in recent weeks has been turned, and properly so, to the forthcoming "missile gap." I have spoken on this floor previously about this gap and the dangers it presents. I intend to address myself to the subject again, but I wish to speak today about a gap which constitutes an equally clear and present danger to our security.

Unlike the missile gap, the gap to which I allude will not reach the point of critical danger in 1961. That point has already been reached.

Unlike the missile gap, the gap to which I refer is not even on the surface being reduced by the combined efforts of our executive and legislative branches. It is, on the contrary, consistently ignored and steadily widening.

Unlike the missile gap, the gap to which I refer gives rise to no speculation as to whether the Russians will exploit it to their advantage and to our detriment. They are exploiting it now.

I am talking about the economic gap, the gap in living standards and income and hope for the future, the gap between the developed and the underdeveloped worlds; between, roughly speaking, the top half of our globe and the bottom half; between the stable, industrialized nations of the north, whether they are friends or foes, and the overpopulated, underinvested nations of the south, whether they are friends or neutrals.

It is this gap which presents us with our most critical challenge today. It is this gap which is altering the face of the globe, our strategy, our security, and our alliances, more than any current military challenge. And it is this economic challenge to which we have responded most sporadically, most timidly, and most inadequately.

[2] From speech by Senator John F. Kennedy (Democrat, Massachusetts), February 19, 1959. *Congressional Record.* 105:2483-7. F. 19, '59.

Since the truce negotiations in Korea began eight years ago, it should have been obvious that our greatest danger was no longer military. Since the Russians began their aid and trade penetration of the underdeveloped world some five years ago, it should have been obvious now that if India were to fall, if Latin America turned away and if the Middle East slid behind the Iron Curtain, then no amount of missiles, no amount of space satellites or nuclear-powered planes or atomic submarines could ever save us.

And yet our response to this economic gap has never equaled our obligation or our opportunity. The problem is neither regional nor temporary—it is global and long range. Our response has sometimes been wasteful in expenditure and grandiloquent in rhetoric—but it has never been global and long range.

We have reacted *ad hoc* to a crisis here and a crisis there, year by year, region by region. When the Latin Americans throw rocks at the Vice President, there is finally talk of a Latin American loan fund. When a friendly monarch is threatened in the Middle East, money is dispersed helter-skelter while there is brave but brief talk about an Arab development fund.

Let there be pressures from a north African nation and there is talk of economic aid to meet that crisis in that nation at that time. Let there be a foreign exchange crisis in India threatening all democratic hope in India and free Asia as a whole—and we bail the Indians out, at an inadequate level, for one year only.

This policy of using money on a crisis basis, from year to year, wherever difficulty arises, is expensive and ineffective. It is wasteful of our funds. It fails to stimulate effective long-range planning and effort by the recipients. It denies us the opportunity to impose meaningful standards for the use of our aid or significant requirements as to what they must do to match it. There is no follow-through, no consistency, no attempt to match our effort to their need and our resources. And so, among the nations of the world, the rich grow richer as the poor grow poorer—with less capital and more people and fewer homes. It is this kind of atmosphere which increases the appeal of a narrow nationalism and dictatorship which argues that economic inter-dependence with foreign nations is ominous. . . .

In . . . [1958] when China may well have increased her over-all food production by one-half, Indian food production rose only by a few bare percentage points. . . . India produced only slightly more than 60 million tons of food grains, yet the minimum annual need for India at the start of her third Five-Year Plan two years from now will be 80 million tons. For the first time in modern history a government appears to have found a way—however brutal its human defects—which appears to solve the problems of large peasant underemployment and labor surplus. The mobilization of the unemployed mass of Chinese rural workers through economic communes, cottage industry, small pig-iron schemes, and all the rest is an achievement whose political and intellectual impact in less developed areas is bound to be immense.

We know that in a nation of stable population which is in the process of economic takeoff a program of investment of at least 8 per cent of national income is necessary, for an annual growth of 2 per cent. But more typically these nations are also areas of great population growth. In countries with annual population increases of 2 to 3 per cent such as India, it requires an additional 6 to 8 per cent of investment if national income growth is not to be offset by the rise in population. During the past year India has had a national growth rate of only 3 per cent, and 2 per cent of this is largely dissipated by population increases. Two years ago India was reaching a national growth rate of nearly 5 per cent, but the cutbacks in her plan and bad harvests have blighted this achievement.

In short, to nations in a hurry to emerge from the rut of underdevelopment, Communist China offers a potential model—1958 was their "round." As their trade and aid offensive mounted, as their own example proved more attractive, our trade and aid programs faltered and our economy stood still—with our recession cutting the price received for commodities the underdeveloped nations must sell, while our inflation continued to boost the prices they paid for our machinery. . . .

I cite India today because of her special importance, representing as she does some 40 per cent of the population in the uncommitted world, representing the one great counter to the ideological and economic forces of Red China, and symbolizing for all Asia the testing ground for democracy under pressure. . . .

I do not say that India could not tread water for a few more years before going under. But . . . the Indians need confidence that they can plan major efforts for long-range progress with some assurance of substantial, long-term assistance from the Western world.

More short-term credit cannot do the job. India now has large amounts of foreign debts, both public and private, which must be repaid in hard currency at the very time a new thrust will be needed to move into its third plan. As long as our efforts are aimed only at assuring short-term solvency, they only leave plans for an effective Indian development program suspended in midair—bringing still closer the hour of disaster.

Congress should, of course, base its aid programs on sound criteria and productive investment. But let us remember economies need time to mature. Our own nation, in the days of its youth, sold railroad bonds to the British and other Europeans—and these were long forty- or fifty-year debentures. With the growth of our productive capacity, we gradually became a creditor nation with the ability to repay these foreign investments. There is no question that the Indians, given proper assurance and assistance, could do the same.

Moreover, the foreign exchange shortage has had the effect of holding back private capitalism in India which had shown unexpected strength. A more secure margin in foreign reserves would give to the private sector its old buoyancy, and break down the outmoded wall between private and public planning and development.

But neither the Indians nor the Americans can achieve any success in these matters if we continue to concentrate obsessively on the size of the Indian deficit and how it can be chipped away little by little. Let us concentrate instead on trying to make a success of a common enterprise which is a sensible program for the next stage of Indian economic growth.

Last year Senator Cooper and I recommended that consideration be given to the creation of an international advisory group representing potential donor nations to examine India's needs and plans, and make precise recommendations to the member governments. The case for such an international consortium is even more compelling this year. We have talked for many years about moving the Western alliance along more constructive channels—about making something more out of it than an anti-Soviet venture. India presents us with such an opportunity—for several Western nations and Japan share a deep concern for the future of that vital area. Canada, Great Britain, Germany, and Japan would, I feel certain, have an interest in joining in a frank and realistic exchange and survey of India's future needs; and in making a proportional sacrifice and commitment to meet those needs.

Such a mission, particularly if it drew upon men of both national and international stature, such as John McCloy of the United States, Sir Oliver Franks of the United Kingdom, and Escott Reid of Canada, would be uniquely effective in providing a fresh approach, avoiding misunderstandings on both sides, encouraging the Indians in their association with the West, stimulating effective, efficient plans and appropriate lending criteria.

Such a donors' club, under the sponsorship of the World Bank, would not cut athwart any existing institutions. On the contrary, it would help to harmonize the individual aid programs of the individual nations, without trying to build a new bureaucratic superstructure. The initiative for such a cooperative examination of India's long-term needs must, of course, come from the Indians, just as the final decision following such consultations must be theirs alone.

Mr. President, I am submitting, together with the distinguished Senator from Kentucky [Mr. Cooper], a concurrent resolution which expresses the interest of Congress in the creation of a free world mission which would canvass India's requirements and make recommendations to participating nations regarding joint means by which they can more effectively support India's economic development efforts. I am delighted that in the House of Representatives Representatives Bowles of Connecticut and Representative Merrow of New Hampshire are submitting the same resolution on a bipartisan basis. . . .

As a nation, we think not of war but of peace; not of crusades of conflict but of covenants of cooperation; not of the pageantry of imperialism but of the pride of new states freshly risen to independence. We like to look, with Mr. Justice Holmes, beyond the vision of battling races and an impoverished earth to catch a dreaming glimpse of peace. In the words of Edmund Burke, we sit on a "conspicuous stage," and the whole world marks our demeanor. In this year and in this Congress we have an opportunity to be worthy of that role.

The concurrent resolution (S. Con. Res. 11), submitted by Mr. Kennedy (for himself and Mr. Cooper), was referred to the Committee on Foreign Relations, as follows:

Whereas the continued vitality and success of the Republic of India is a matter of common free world interest, politically because of her 400 million people and vast land area; strategically because of her commanding geographic location; economically because of her organized national development effort; and morally because of her heartening commitment to the goals, values, and institutions of democracy: Now, therefore, be it

Resolved by the Senate (the House of Representatives concurring), That it is the sense of Congress that the United States Government should invite other friendly and democratic nations to join in a mission to consult with India on the detailed possibilities for joint action to assure the fulfillment of India's second 5-year plan and the effective design of its third plan.

And that the Secretary of State report to the Congress on the feasibility of such a mission after consultation with interested Governments and with the Republic of India.

[This resolution was later broadened, at the suggestion of the State Department, to refer to southern Asia in general and as thus revised was approved by Congress.—Ed.]

IN SUPPORT OF AID [3]

The current [1958] Indian foreign exchange crisis has arisen for a reason which should cheer . . . us all. It has arisen because the unexpected momentum of the private-enterprise sector of the Indian economy exhausted the foreign exchange budgeted for it over a five-year period in about eighteen months.

Why, then, should not the Indian government withdraw from the economic scene? Why are more intergovernmental loans needed?

Indian government investment, backed by enlarged inter-governmental loans, is needed for precisely the same reason that our state and Federal governments had to take a hand in American economic development a century or so ago, for precisely the same reason that we needed to import vast amounts of foreign capital in the nineteenth century: to build economic overhead capital, notably, in our case, the railroads and other means of transport. We do not now have the private international bond market which permitted the governments of developing countries to borrow for this purpose before 1914.

If industry is to expand in India it requires that the Indian railroads, electric power supply, road system, etc., expand. These things cannot be accomplished by private enterprise alone any more than the Erie Canal could have been built by American private enterprise in the 1820's or the transcontinental railroads without heavy Federal subsidy in the form of land grants.

I . . . hope that India will emerge with a system of decentralized economic power to match its political democracy. That outcome depends, however, on the success of the government of India in building the framework for a modern industrial system over the next five to ten years.

The frustration of this effort due to a lack of foreign exchange will not lead to decentralization, unless it is to the kind of decentralization to be observed now in the chaos of Indonesia. It will lead to that higher degree of authoritarianism which the

[3] From "Aid to India Supported," letter to editor, April 12, 1958, by W. W. Rostow, economic historian. New York *Times.* p 22. Ap. 21, '58. Reprinted by permission.

Communist party of India aims to dominate, if and when the
Indian second Five-Year Plan fails.

For this reason, despite the ample and urgent distractions of
American political life at the moment, the Cooper-Kennedy proposal deserves to be taken seriously.

AGAINST AID [4]

One of the least attractive features of United States foreign
aid is that it goes to governments. It helps them build not only
"public works" like dams and roads but also engage in business
activities which are the normal sphere of private enterprise.

Thus, ironically enough, scores of billions of dollars earned
by Americans in a free economy have been busily subsidizing the
spread of socialism, particularly in so-called "underdeveloped"
lands. . . .

The Indian government, it seems, is finding itself in fresh
economic difficulties [1957]. If the big American loan is not
forthcoming, it is suggested, the second Five-Year Plan may have
to be cut drastically. In that event the country may be pushed
into even more of a managed economy than it now has, with
further losses of political freedom.

Yet the curious thing is that the Indian government has
already received hundreds of millions of dollars worth of American loans and grants and is still getting such aid at the rate of
about $60 million a year. It evidently has not accomplished
much, since the symptom of India's present trouble is a sharp
drop in foreign exchange reserves.

A huge new United States loan, then, could hardly solve
anything. . . . For India's difficulties stem from overambitious
state planning in a "mixed" economy based on socialism. When
the second Five-Year Plan was unveiled, economists noted that it
was full of inflationary potential and was generally unrealistic.

That is the kind of drain down which American dollars can
be poured endlessly without ever improving the standard of living of the Indian people. It is not pleasant to conjecture how

[4] "Subsidizing Socialism," editorial. *Wall Street Journal.* p 12. S. 16, '57.
Reprinted by permission.

much actual harm has been done, in India and elsewhere, by America's tremendous investment in the exploded economics of socialism.

Whatever the present policy may be, we hope the government will have sense enough to turn down the request of India or any similar request. But the only way to make sure that dollars no longer buttress socialism is to bring to a halt the whole program of indiscriminate and unthinking handouts.

FOREIGN AID AND INVESTMENT [5]

External Aid to India From Other Nations

(1949 Through April 15, 1959)

UNITED STATES		$ 1,711,000,000
Wheat Loan	$ 189.7 Million	
Public Law 480	664.0 Million	
Export-Import Bank	152.0 Million	
Development Loan Fund ..	175.0 Million	
ICA, TC and other loans ..	150.0 Million	
Grants	380.0 Million	
INTERNATIONAL AGENCIES		732,000,000
World Bank	532.0 Million	
International Monetary Fund	200.0 Million	
OTHER FREE WORLD NATIONS		715,000,000
United Kingdom	186.0 Million	
West Germany	257.0 Million	
Japan	68.0 Million	
Canada	176.0 Million	
Australia and New Zealand	26.0 Million	
Norway	2.0 Million	
SOVIET BLOC AID		304,000,000
TOTAL		$ 3,462,000,000

1. The UN spent $6.5 million on technical assistance projects in India and the UNICEF spent $6.8 million during a four year period, 1954-1957.

    [5] From *Economic World.* 1:A-1; 5. My. '59.

2. In the fiscal year 1958 American voluntary agencies shipped $10.8 million worth of surplus food to India including wheat, corn meal and dried milk on which International Cooperation Administration paid ocean freight of $3 million. These agencies also sent medical supplies, vitamins, and other food in the amount of $200,000.

3. India provided about 91 per cent of the total cost of financing the first Five-Year Plan from her own resources and about 9 per cent came from external assistance.

Private Foreign Investment in India

The estimated total of foreign private capital investment in India at the end of 1958 was $1,340,000,000.

Of this total about $110,000,000 represented new private American capital invested in India since 1949. However, some sources place the American figure as high as $150,000,000 to $200,000,000 if reinvested profits and dividends are also included. American private investments, which have tripled in value since India's independence, have risen from a total of $38,000,000 in 1950.

Total foreign investment in the private sector in 1958 was $11,807,880. Of this figure, U. S. investors provided $4,179,000; Italian — $2,856,000; United Kingdom — $2,203,740; Swiss — $2,184,000; and Japanese, $378,000.

A Reserve Bank of India report up to the end of 1955 gave a total of $1,008,000,000 for all foreign private investments. Of this figure, over 81 per cent, or $819,000,000 represented the investments of United Kingdom businessmen. American investments amounted to approximately 10 per cent of this figure, or $84,000,000.

Private investors of other nations as of 1955 were: Switzerland $13,860,000, Pakistan $10,900,000, Germany $5,250,000 Japan $5,250,000, Canada $3,150,000.

Sources: Government of India, International Monetary Fund.

U.S. FOOD SURPLUSES FOR INDIA [6]

When S. K. Patil, India's new Minister of Food and Agriculture, goes to the United States in November [1959] with a brave new plan for solving this country's formidable food problem, his political future may be at stake. Patil's objective, basically, is to persuade the United States government to store a part of its huge grain surplus in India, thereby doing a service to India and perhaps also to the American taxpayer. . . .

[In mid-1959] he took on what is probably the toughest and most thankless political assignment in India. Nobody has ever profited politically from accepting the portfolio of food and agriculture. The most recent incumbent, A. P. Jain, tossed in the sponge under a barrage of parliamentary criticism. But Patil was not easily scared. . . .

There is no place in the Indian government where Patil's dynamic qualities are more needed than in the food ministry, which had become bogged down in bureaucratic red tape and administrative inefficiency. India had been importing food grains at the rate of 3 million tons annually to meet her deficit. She had just experienced her best crop in years. Basically there was no reason for shortages in the marketplace. Yet in many places food prices had shot up unreasonably and the system of state trading had proved ineffective. The recent bloody rioting in Calcutta shows what can happen when the food situation is exploited by political extremists.

Much of India's trouble, Patil points out, is attributable to the chronologically narrow margin between the reserves of food grains and the amount required to meet public demand. This provides hoarders, speculators and profiteers with a fine opportunity to manipulate the market to their own advantage. The solution, says Patil, is to build up a large enough stockpile of grain to ensure a "dependable margin" of supply over demand. He proposes that the United States government assist in establishing such a reserve in India—a reserve of food grains that would be maintained at not less than 5 million tons for a period

[6] From "India and U.S. Food Surpluses," by A. T. Steele, foreign correspondent. New York *Herald Tribune.* p 24. O. 21, '59. Reprinted by permission

of from five to ten years. Such a reserve would put a sure-fire check on high prices, Patil believes.

As Patil envisions it, at least 4 million tons of the stockpile would consist of wheat and about one million tons of rice, with most of the wheat, at least, coming from the United States. He would also like to stockpile about 250,000 tons of sugar. At present India has storage facilities for only 2 million tons of grain, but Patil is confident the Indian government could increase storage capacity to 5 million tons within a couple of years. He would finance the building of these facilities with borrowings from the large rupee credit which the United States has accumulated in this country. Grain stored in India by the American government under the Patil plan would remain United States property until drawn upon, when it would be bought by India on the same basis as other surplus purchases.

The whole scheme is designed of course to stabilize India's difficult food problem without any additional expenditure of foreign exchange, every cent of which is needed for implementation of the Five-Year Plan. Patil believes his bold grain storage plan could be worked out through United States Public Law 480, the legislation under which India is obtaining most of her grain imports at the present time. Under this law surplus American commodities are sold to countries like India on easy terms in their own currencies. . . .

Patil is of the opinion that within ten years India should have her food problem pretty well licked. But that will depend on a more rapid increase in agricultural production than has been achieved up to now. Patil holds that stabilization of farm prices through his storage program will give the peasants fresh incentive. Intensive efforts to build up farm output are projected under the third Five-Year Plan.

AN AMERICAN VIEW [7]

The best news out of India today is that her leaders are finally aware of the menace of Communist China.

[7] From *A Report from India and Pakistan*, by Averell Harriman. North American Newspaper Alliance. Chicago. '59. p 3-8. Reprinted by permission of the author and North American Newspaper Alliance, Inc.

Impressed by communism's achievements but repelled by its methods, they are now facing up to the fact that the world's most populous democracy is in crucial competition with the world's most populous dictatorship. Either they or the Chinese will become the model for Asia's awakening peoples. . . .

This sense of urgency in the competition is not only something new in India (it was not so long ago that Mr. Nehru expressed fraternal praise of Communist China), but it is one of several factors that have gradually mellowed Indian attitudes toward the United States. . . . I fully agree with India's ambassador to Washington, who recently said that "our relations have never been better." . . .

What has happened is that India's leaders, increasingly aware of their identity with the democratic world, are today less inclined to find fault with every aspect of our sometimes misguided foreign policy.

I think there are at least four factors—apart from the concern over China—that have softened Indian feelings about the United States in the last two or three years:

First, we have been fortunate in that our two ambassadors during this period—John Sherman Cooper and Ellsworth Bunker—are the kind of men Indians like and respect.

Second, there have been fewer careless statements out of Washington—such as Secretary of State Dulles' ill-considered remark about Goa. [In December, 1955, Secretary Dulles and the Portuguese Foreign Minister issued a statement referring to "Portugal's provinces in the Far East." The Indian government interpreted this as meaning the United States supported Portugal's claim that Goa, a settlement on the west coast of the Indian subcontinent, is a province of Portugal. The Indian position is that Goa is a colony held by force. Officially, the United States position on Goa has always been neutral.]

And there is a more understanding attitude by our press of India's problems and sensitivities. At the same time, first hand reports by Indian visitors to the United States have helped dispel some of the myths about United States "materialism."

Third, the Soviet Union's brutal intervention in Hungary—and the murder of Imre Nagy—shocked many Indians into realizing what Soviet colonialism means.

Fourth, our relatively modest but timely economic aid—mostly loans with no strings attached—has favorably impressed Indian leaders who were formerly suspicious of our motives.

Perhaps I should also mention that after twelve years of independence, India's leaders are more sure of themselves (and therefore less sensitive to criticism) and better able to appreciate their friends in the West now that time has cooled the left-over passions of colonial days.

Problems India Faces

With this new political maturity has come the realization that Americans, more than most people, are in a position to understand what Nehru . . . [calls] the "tremendous adventure" of building up a new nation by democratic means.

But these first, encouraging impressions of a country I had not seen since 1946—the year before independence—should not obscure the fact that India is beset by social, economic and political problems that fairly stagger the imagination. This is a nation where 4 out of 5 people can still not read or write.

It is a country short of technicians, short of capital, short of nearly everything except people. And people are increasing about half as fast again as food production: despite government-backed programs of birth control, there are 6 million more Indians to be fed, housed, clothed and employed every year.

That is why India is a nation desperately in need of assistance if her tremendous adventure is not to end in tremendous tragedy. In her race with Communist China, which has received massive Soviet aid topped by a 5 billion-ruble loan . . . [in 1959], India has certain advantages—vigorous and determined leadership, a well-trained civil service, world-renowned scientists, a good railroad system and a fledgling industrial base, undamaged by war, on which to build.

Her big disadvantage is that the democratic methods of education and persuasion are not as quick as those of a ruthless dictatorship in achieving the spectacular production increases that Asians are being told to expect.

India's progress is steady and impressive. Thanks to the Community Development Program, life in one half of the nation's 500,000 villages is brighter after many years of darkness. But the ambitious goals of the second Five-Year Plan are not being met, and the third will flounder without substantial injections of foreign capital.

As Vice President Sarvepalli Radhakrishan told me, "We are moving in the right direction, but our pace is far too slow." . . .

Soviet Successes in India

In less than two years, a task force of Russian engineers in pith helmets and khaki work clothes has helped transform . . . [Bhilai] in central India from a drowsy cluster of huts to a booming industrial community of 65,000 steel and construction workers.

They are assisting in the construction of a steel mill that is already producing pig iron and that by 1961 will have a capacity of a million tons of steel, or one sixth of the nation's planned output.

To make this project possible, the Soviet government loaned India about half the total cost—$140 million (at 2.5 per cent interest)—for the purchase of Russian equipment, and sent in 800 engineers and technicians who knew from experience at home or in China how to put up a modern steel plant from scratch.

As in China, these Russians have not tried to run the show; instead, they act as advisers and instructors to the Indian staff officially in charge. The result has been a smooth-working partnership based on mutual respect.

I talked at length with both Indians and Russians. The latter, with their wives and children, now number some 1,500. Relations seemed cordial but not intimate. (There is not much socializing). These conscientious Russians were frankly homesick—they don't care for the hot climate—and eager to get on with the job. But they and the Indians shared a mutual enthusiasm for "our steel mill" that transcended differences in political ideology.

Bhilai is a vivid symbol of India's determination to industrialize as rapidly as possible. It is also a symbol of Russia's decision to participate in India's development in a spectacular way. Although Soviet aid to India so far amounts to less than one fifth of America's $1.6 billion worth of grants and credits, they are selecting projects, like Bhilai, that make headlines.

For example, the quiet and continuing efforts of United States agricultural experts to increase food production never receive the kind of publicity that the Russians get each time an Indian official cuts a ribbon to dedicate one of their new blast furnaces.

American aid is certainly appreciated by India's top leaders—who know how our shipments of food grains averted hunger and a serious inflation . . . [in 1958]—but its impact on the people can be judged by recent public opinion polls that show that a considerable number of Indians now think their biggest benefactor is the Soviet Union.

It can be argued that India is trying to do too much too soon, and that the emphasis right now should be less on building steel mills that employ relatively few people and more on increasing food production. The per capita daily calorie intake is only about 1,800. This is far too little, particularly in a nation where machines have not yet replaced muscles. And the population is growing at the rate of 6 million a year.

Steel Is a Symbol

But the argument is academic. The decision has been taken by India's planners to develop heavy industry. Two good crops a few years ago may have led them to . . . [underestimate] the food problem, but in any case it would have been hard to resist the glamour of steel—which has become a symbol of economic independence in underdeveloped countries.

Thus, thanks to the Bhilai project, to two other government plants going up with British and German help and to expansion of the great Tata works and other privately owned mills, India will soon be able to boast of a 6 million-ton-a-year steel industry, evenly divided between the private and public sectors.

For those who deduce from official statements that India is heading toward full nationalization, I might add that 90 per cent of the industrial output outside of public utilities is still in private hands.

The men in charge of planning India's economic future told me that home-produced steel was essential for general industrial development and much-needed jobs for the millions of chronically unemployed. For instance, steel produced at Bhilai will be cheaper than imported steel and will save India $150 a ton in scarce foreign exchange.

As for food production, they point out that, with steel and heavy industry, India can build more fertilizer plants like the one I saw at Sindri, which already furnishes one third of the nation's present minimum needs.

India now requires a million additional tons of food grains each year—or $100 million worth of imports—just to take care of her population increase. They estimate that these requirements can be more than met by building a $44 million fertilizer plant each year for the next five years.

The goal of the planners is to achieve a "breakthrough" by the end of the third five-year plan in 1966 that will not only double India's average per capita annual income of $56, but transform Indian, in Nehru's phrase, "from an underdeveloped to a self-developing nation"—that is, a prospering nation capable of obtaining its foreign exchange through trade and normal channels of credit and investment.

The five-year plans may be over-ambitious; the second one is already running about 15 per cent behind schedule. But you cannot blame those responsible for India's future for setting their sights high, and keeping them high. The plans not only spell out the kind of progress India's people are demanding from their government, but also give them something to look forward to.

Already, after only twelve years of independence, you can see everywhere that India's 400 million people are astir. In the villages, the dedication of the young Community Development officials is inspiring; and the new brick construction rising among the mud huts is a sign that farmers, no longer under the landlord's yoke, are developing a feeling of ownership and self-reliance.

Touring the Damodar Valley in eastern India, the source of 90 per cent of the nation's coking coal, I was much impressed by the new dams and factories that are creating power, jobs, flood control and tillable land affecting millions of people. (Also impressive are the modern housing projects being erected by both private and public enterprises.) This Indian version of our TVA is costing $250 million, but like its American model it will prove to be a priceless investment.

Meanwhile, it is no secret that India is desperately short of foreign exchange to tide her over the critical next few years until the "breakthrough."

Capital is hard to raise in a country where fewer than 500,000 families have taxable incomes above $600 a year, and where 200 million live on no more than 10 cents a day. Capital has little chance to accumulate. In spite of that, most of the cost of the new development comes from Indian resources.

I asked India's top economic experts what they would need in loans from all countries to fulfill their plans. Estimates varied from $2 billion to $4 billion, spread over the third Five-Year Plan—preferably in long-term credits to make possible the import of required capital goods. (I am inclined to believe the higher figure is closer to the need, if only because pride and enthusiasm tend to make the experts underestimate their nation's problems.)

This is a lot of money. But it is still only 10 to 20 per cent of the plan's projected costs. And with neighboring—and competitive—Red China, making its "great leap forward" through regimentation and the help of Soviet loans, India cannot afford to be leisurely about the future.

How far is the Soviet Union prepared to underwrite India's development as well? I hear it is negotiating to build plants to make heavy machinery, optical glass and pharmaceuticals in different parts of India, just as it is now building Bhilai and it expects to reap dividends of good will for itself and prestige for the Indian Communist party.

This is the sort of competition the West is up against in India. Our disadvantage is the same as India's disadvantage vis-à-vis China: Democracies cannot move as swiftly (or as ruthlessly) as dictatorships.

When the Kremlin leaders were told by the Indian ambassador that India had to have wheat to avert a famine in 1951, they were loading grain ships within forty-eight hours; our government had been "studying" the question for months.

The fact that we later sent India twenty times as much wheat as did the Russians is not generally understood; they got the headlines.

India is a nation on the march. No visitor can fail to be impressed by the zeal with which her leaders are trying to overcome staggering economic and social problems. But zeal alone is not enough, for India's economy is like a plane taking off from a newly built runway: it can't afford to lose momentum or altitude.

INDIA, THE GLORIOUS GAMBLE [8]

We have now been engaged in the cold war for some ten years, and we know many things today that we did not know when it began. One of them is the subject of this article. It is that what happens in India during the next ten years will be of critical importance in the great conflict generated by the rise of communism.

Ten years ago, in the years immediately following the second World War, the critical area of the world was Western Europe. Great Britain, France, Western Germany, Italy and the Low Countries were prostrated and exhausted, bankrupt and without

[8] Article by Walter Lippmann, columnist. *Ladies' Home Journal*. 76:48-9. Ag. '59. Reprinted by permission. Copyright 1959 The Curtis Publishing Company.

defenses. Worst of all, they were unable by their own efforts to rebuild their ruins and to revive their economies, and thus they were without hope. This crisis—which threatened to bring about the downfall of Western civilization in Europe—was met in this country by two very great acts of statesmanship. One was the Marshall Plan; the other was the organization of NATO. These two acts made it possible for Western Europe to recover from the war, and to become, by its own hard work and know-how, the second most productive area in the world.

But in the very years when we were making it possible for Western Europe to bring about its own recovery, the Western position and influence in China collapsed. Whether this could have been prevented has been hotly debated in this country. The fact is that China now is a Communist country, and that there is no practical prospect whatever that the Communists who rule China can be ousted from abroad or overthrown from within.

The Red Chinese government is working with a fierce and fanatical energy to overcome the immemorial poverty and backwardness of the Chinese nation. It is a terrible and awe-inspiring spectacle, which rests on this fundamental thesis: that in order to raise the great masses of Asia out of their primitive way of life, it is necessary to sacrifice the lives of many, and the comforts of most, of a whole generation of the Chinese people.

Is this necessary? Is this the only way? Must a backward people choose between remaining backward and submitting to an ordeal of tyranny and of cruelty in order to get over the hump and into the modern age? On the answer to these questions depends, we had better realize, the future of Southern Asia, of the Middle East, and of Africa, and, it may well be, of a part of Latin America.

These questions cannot be answered by generalities; as, for example, by declaring that our democratic system of free enterprise is better than the Communist system. We must teach ourselves to understand that our system, which grew up on a rich and empty continent, cannot be duplicated in Asia. Because of that, though the picture of our material prosperity is admired and envied, it is in fact readily exploited for Communist propaganda. For what the Communists say is that in the over-crowded and backward countries they alone have a way of lift-ing the people within sight of an American standard of life. They point to Russia and say they can prove their claim by what has been done there in the past forty years.

The influence of communism in the underdeveloped coun-tries of the world lies, above all else, in the example of Russia—in the demonstration that in forty years a defeated and backward country, which had to fight a civil war and a world war as well, has become one of the two mightiest powers in the world.

You cannot, as they say, beat a horse with no horse. We cannot beat the Soviet example by our example. For we are not an example that backward peoples can follow, and unless we can manage to create an example which they can follow, we shall almost certainly lose the cold war in Asia and Africa, and perhaps elsewhere.

There will be some, I know, who will say: Why is it our business to create an example which the backward peoples can follow? Do we not have enough problems of our own to worry us without taking on any responsibility for solving the problems of the great masses of backward peoples?

The answer to these questions is that we can no more with-draw from the world community than an American family can withdraw from the community in which it lives. Least of all can a family withdraw if it happens to be, as we are in the world, the richest member of the community. It is impossible to say: My children go to a private school. Why should I pay school taxes for the public schools? It is impossible to say: I go about in my private automobile. Why should I care about buses and streetcars and subways? For the same reason, the United States cannot make itself richer and richer, and not care what happens elsewhere. We cannot do this because if we did those of us who have a conscience would have a bad con-science. And even if we did not have a bad conscience, it would be frightening to live in a world in which we had aroused the envy and had provoked the hatred of so large a part of mankind.

There is, however, so it seems to me, an even greater reason than these. It is that we have the opportunity—indeed, we may call it a privilege—of playing a leading part in a noble and fascinating and decisive human adventure. The age we live in, this twentieth century, is the beginning of many things, and of these the most important is the awakening and the uprising of the submerged masses in the old imperial lands.

It is an uprising not only against foreign domination, but also against their own native feudalism or tribalism and above all against their abject poverty. We could not, of course, control this historic movement even if we tried. But what we may be able to do is to assist in a demonstration for all the world to see of how, without the sacrifice of human rights, it may be possible to conquer poverty.

We come now to the practical question of where this demonstration can best be made, and of how it can be made.

It can best be made in India. Why in India? First of all, because the demonstration must be made in a big country. Russia is a big country and China is a big country. And what we have to do is to demonstrate that poverty can be conquered in a big country. We have already proved in Puerto Rico what can be done in a small country which has a rich friend. Puerto Rico is inspiring. But it does not prove the point that has to be proved: that the standard of life can be raised decisively in a very big and a very poor country.

The second reason for choosing India for this demonstration is that if India turns to communism, as almost surely it will if it fails in its present plans of development, Asia will be dominated by three Communist powers—the Soviet Union, China and India.

As things are going now in India, the rate of progress is so slow that for all practical human purposes there is no progress at all. The Indian economy is at present growing at a rate of about 4 per cent a year. We must not be misled by the fact that this rate of growth is in fact faster than our own. That is a statistical illusion. For the Indian economy is so appallingly poor that if it grows only at the rate of 4 per cent a year, it will take thirty-five years to increase the Indian per capita income to just over two dollars a week. If that is the best that can be done, there will be a political disaster in India before the thirty-five years are over.

The third reason for choosing India is that India now has enough technical ability, enough competence in organization, in management and in administration. Enough for what? Enough to use successfully an amount of foreign aid that will make possible within the next eight to fifteen years India's transition from economic stagnation to a condition of sustained economic growth.

The aim of India, as for any of the industrially underdeveloped countries, is to reach as quickly as possible the point of "economic take-off" from which point on it can sustain its own further economic growth through its own surplus of capital and the normal channels of international investment.

Until this stage of development has been reached, India will require outside aid. It is estimated that India's need will be for between $8 billion and $10 billion of foreign exchange before it can reach the point of economic take-off.

As a first step toward this goal, India is now preparing a third Five-Year Plan which envisions a total capital investment of $20 billion from 1961 to 1966. One fourth of this amount— $5 billion—is required in foreign exchange and must come from such outside sources as the private-capital markets of the Western world, the World Bank and foreign governments. It is this effort to obtain $1 billion a year from outside sources that the United States will want to support.

The third Five-Year Plan is designed to develop the sectors of India's economy that are crucial to its further development. The capital investment will be in agriculture, chiefly to build dams to provide water, and factories to provide fertilizer. It will also be in the development of oil, in steel, in the nonferrous metals, in heavy machinery and in the further development of coal, electric power and transport.

If the Five-Year Plan can fulfill its objectives, India in 1966 will be within a few years of achieving self-sufficiency, of having become an independent, self-generating economy. It will be close to its goal. It will be close to that point in its development where it will need no foreign capital beyond what can be obtained by normal commercial operations and private foreign investment.

This can be done, as I said above, because India already has the administrative capacity to carry out successfully a large and sustained program of economic development. India is a frightfully poor country. But it is not backward, as are many countries in Africa, for example, where the masses are still living in the Stone Age and where society is still tribal. In India there is an educated class in government and in industry which is quite capable, if, for the next few years, it has some material help from the outside, of accomplishing the take-off from the ancient stagnant poverty of Asia toward a progressive, independent, modern economy.

This is what Russia has accomplished in the past forty years. This is what China may be accomplishing now.

Nobody can guarantee that India will succeed. The honest thing to say is that the odds are not unfavorable, and that what is asked of us in money is not very much, considering what we and all the world may win from making the attempt. What is asked of us is the better part of a billion dollars a year for the next five to ten years. This is less than one ninth of our present investment in surplus crops which we do not know what to do with.

To be sure, a billion dollars is a lot of money and even the United States cannot afford to throw it away carelessly. But a billion dollars a year for a few years to help India make the take-off may be, if the experiment and the demonstration succeed, as good a gamble as this country has taken since Jefferson made the Louisiana Purchase and Seward bought Alaska. For if India can rise out of the stagnant morass of Asian poverty without resorting to the totalitarian method, we shall see one of the very great moments of the age we live in.

It will have been proved to all the world that there is another way to conquer poverty than that which is now being used in

Russia and in China. If there is such another way, a resounding blow will have been struck for the cause of freedom.

When I think of this glorious gamble which is offered to us, I think of what is the alternative to our taking this monetary risk. If we will not make the contribution, what then? The answer is that in all probability there will set in a great despair in India, and in this despair the Communist alternative will find little resistance.

By failing now to respond to India's need, to meet this stirring challenge, we shall deprive India of choice. We shall, in effect, be asking India to sacrifice a whole generation to the totalitarian alternative. We shall be saying that we cannot afford to demonstrate that a democratic solution is possible.

If that happens because we do not understand the issue, just what, I ask myself, will we have been doing with the dollars which we refused to spend on the great gamble?

THE PRESIDENT SPEAKS IN INDIA [9]

Talk at Reception

My good friends:

Your President and Prime Minister told me several days ago a half million of you would gather here today. I hardly realized then how impressive and moving and inspiring a sight you would actually be.

Now I know. And I thank you from my heart for the labor you have imposed on yourselves; the miles you have traveled; the hours you have waited in patience. I thank you for all the personal sacrifice and civic effort that a reception like this requires.

I see in the magnificent spectacle before me a soul-stirring testimonial by half a million of India's people to America, a sister democracy—and to the cause for which both India and America stand: The cause of peace and friendship in freedom.

The critical word and key idea of this cause is: freedom.

[9] Text of two speeches by President Eisenhower as reprinted in the New York Times. p 12. D. 14, '59.

We, of these two peaceful nations, believe there are greater things in the world even than peace. They are the ideals, hopes and aspirations of humanity; our loyalty to conscience. They are the integrity of purpose, unswerving devotion to principle, love of truth and decency. The people who believe and practice these things are certain to be friends.

Above all, we believe that only in freedom can men enjoy true and full peace; only in freedom can men be genuine and honest friends. Freedom must come first, we of India and America believe. One of the clearest voices of all time, proclaiming the priority and supremacy of freedom, is your own sainted Mahatma Gandhi.

Speaking of freedom for the nations he said: "Freedom is a gift of God—the right of every nation."

And to his words America replies: So also we believe.

Speaking of freedom for individuals he said: "Democracy is not a state in which people act like sheep. Under democracy individual liberty of opinion and action is jealously guarded."

And to his words America answers: So also we hold.

And then speaking of responsibility, political freedom and the demands of those who possess it, he said: "Self-government depends entirely upon our own internal strength, upon our ability to fight against the heaviest odds. Indeed self-government which does not require continuous striving to attain it and to sustain it is not worth the name." And to his words America can say: So also we teach.

In what I have quoted from Mahatma Gandhi I know he spoke the convictions of the American people as clearly as he spoke for India.

We, like you, have won freedom and we strive to assure every individual American of the fullness of responsible freedoms.

America's right, our obligations, for that matter, to maintain a respectable establishment for defense—our duty to join in company with like-thinking peoples for mutual self defense—would, I am sure, be recognized and upheld by the most saintly of men.

Being strong and free, confident that we shall remain strong and free, we are prepared to devote ourselves as a nation—our energies and our talents—to the cause of peace and friendship.

We believe freedom ultimately will be won everywhere. The human hunger for it is far too deep-seated in human nature to be put off by a contrived definition of a man-made philosophy.

Freedom, as Gandhi said, is a gift of God. And God's gift cannot forever be kept from his children.

But—and immediately, instantly—we must search out with all free nations more effective and practical ways to strengthen the cause of peace and friendship in freedom; and so doing, make our negotiations with other people more persuasive.

One reason I came to India is to tell you America wants to join with all free men in advancing this cause.

Between the first largest democracy on earth, India, and the second largest, America, lie ten thousand miles of land and ocean. But in our fundamental ideas and convictions about democracy we are close neighbors. We ought to be closer.

We who are free, and who prize our freedom above all other gifts of God and nature, must know each other better, trust each other more, support each other.

A free India and a free America could not exist if they were isolated from others in the world. A free society of nations can continue to exist only as it meets the rightful demands of people for security, progress and increasing opportunity for betterment for themselves and their children.

Such a society, if some of its nations prosper richly and others barely feed their people, cannot survive.

When I consider in my own mind the potential contribution of India to the prosperity of its own people and of the entire free world—say in the next ten years—my imagination fails me.

Here will be almost half a billion free men and women well embarked on economic expansion.

The productivity of your farmers will have increased enormously—I saw clear signs of that at the World Agriculture Fair.

Their standards of living will rise. You will be turning out textiles, metals, manufactured goods to help meet the multiplied demands of a world ever growing in its economic appetite.

You will be building houses, schools, hospitals, places of worship, centers for recreation to add culture on a scale possibly never before dreamed of, even here. And you will be doing this without abandoning your freedom in favor of forced regimentation.

As you prosper, the whole free world will prosper. Americans, Asians, Africans, Europeans will buy goods from India they must have to meet their own increasing requirements—that they themselves cannot meet at all or so well. You will be able to buy more from them. A spiral of prosperity throughout the free world will lift the living standards of all our peoples.

Of course I don't think India can achieve its full potential without the acquisition of more capital than you now possess.

The best means for a nation determined to maintain independence are private investment from outside, governmental loans and, where necessary, grants from other free and friendly nations.

One thing I assure you. From now on I shall be quick to speak out on every possible occasion that India is becoming one of the great investment opportunities of our time—an investment in the strengthening of freedom, in the prosperity of the world.

India, mighty in the numbers of its people and their will to build an ever greater republic, marches—I'm confident—to a great destiny.

[In part as a result of the President's trip, early in 1960 the Administration recommended a 50 per cent increase in aid to India during the next fiscal year.—Ed.]

Farewell Speech

I welcome the privilege of speaking through your radios to bid you farewell. I leave India reluctantly.

My visit here has been one of the moving experiences of my life. During these five days I have met with your distinguished President, with your eminent Prime Minister, with many other of your great leaders. I have felt the warmth and friendship of multitudes of you wherever I have gone. More importantly, I have sensed the spirit of New India; heir to the culture of ages old, now possessed by a grand vision, advancing decisively, building a great modern democracy on the foundation of an ancient civilization.

India filled these past five days of my life with so much challenge, excitement and wonder I shall never forget them.

Some similarities between our two countries have become clear to me.

India and America believe in the dignity of the individual, in each one's right to live his life in his own way. We both believe in equality of opportunity. We both believe in the right of minorities to have their opinions respected and protected. We both believe in the rule of law in world affairs and in the peaceful settlement of international disputes, be they great or small.

These are, indeed, fundamental bonds between us.

You are a very old civilization with an ancient tradition and culture. We are a young country. Our tradition is, as traditions go, young also. But in another sense, in the sense of your independent nationhood, you, too, are young. You are starting as we did 184 years ago on the path of development of a new nation. Your problems are different. Your difficulties are different.

The resources with which you have to work are different. But your purpose is the same as ours was and still is: to develop a country in which every man and woman may have the opportunity in freedom to work out for himself in his own way a rich and satisfying life, a country in which, as Abraham Lincoln said, government is of the people, by the people and for the people.

I have been deeply impressed by the way in which you are shouldering the immense problem of raising the standard of living of your people, by the energy and skill and imagination which you are applying to this task. Your achievements in the twelve years of your independence have been remarkable and promise even more for the future.

I am leaving India with a reinforced conviction that the people of India and the people of the United States are engaged in a common quest for the improvement of the general welfare of their people and for peace with justice throughout the world.

So as I leave I take away the warmest and friendliest feelings for this great nation. I want to thank you again for the welcome which you have extended to me. On behalf of the people of the United States I want to wish you good fortune and success.

BIBLIOGRAPHY

An asterisk (*) preceding a reference indicates that the article or a part of it has been reprinted in this book.

BOOKS AND PAMPHLETS

Bondurant, J. V. and Fisher, Margaret. Indian approaches to a Socialist society. University of California Press. Berkeley. '56.

Bowles, Chester. Ambassador's report. Harper. New York. '54.

Bowles, Cynthia. At home in India. Harcourt. New York. '56.

Brecher, Michael. India's foreign policy. American Institute of Pacific Relations. New York. '57.

Brecher, Michael. Nehru: a political biography. Oxford University Press. New York. '59.

Brown, Norman. United States and India and Pakistan. Harvard University Press. Cambridge, Mass. '55.

Campbell, Alexander. Heart of India. Knopf. New York. '58.

Coale, A. J. and Hoover, E. M. Population growth, an economic development in low-income countries; a case study of India's prospects Princeton University. Princeton, N.J. '58.

*Dean, V. M. Nature of the non-Western world. (Mentor Book) New American Library. New York. '57.

Dean, V. M. New patterns of democracy in India. Harvard University Press. Cambridge, Mass. '59.

De Bary, W. T. and others. Sources of Indian tradition. Columbia University Press. New York. '58.

Dube, S. C. India's changing villages. Cornell University Press. Ithaca, N.Y. '55.

Fischer, Louis. Gandhi: his life and message for the world. New American Library. New York. '54.

Fischer, Louis. Life of Mahatma Gandhi. Harper. New York. '50.

Gandhi, M. K. All men are brothers; life and thoughts of Mahatma Gandhi as told in his own words. UNESCO. Paris. '58.

Gandhi, M. K. Autobiography; my experiments with truth. Beacon. Boston. '57.

Griffiths, Sir Percival. Modern India. Praeger. New York. '57.

*Harriman, W. A. Report from India and Pakistan. North American Newspaper Alliance. Chicago. '59.

Harrison, Selig. India: the dangerous decades. Princeton University Press. Princeton, N.J. '60.

India Planning Commission. New India: progress through democracy. Macmillan. New York. '58.

Isaacs, H. R. Scratches on our minds. Day. New York. '58.

Kautsky, J. H. Moscow and the Communist party in India. Wiley. New York. '56.

Korbel, Josef. Danger in Kashmir. Princeton University Press. Princeton, N.J. '54.

Lewis, Oscar. Village life in northern India. University of Illinois Press. Urbana. '58.

Lin, Yu-t'ang, ed. Wisdom of China and India. Random House. New York. '42.

Malenbaum, Wilfred. East and West in India's development. National Planning Association. Washington, D.C. '59.

Marriott, McKim, ed. Village India: studies in the little community. University of Chicago Press. Chicago. '55.

Masani, M. R. Communist party of India. Macmillan. New York. '54.

Mayer, Albert and others. Pilot project in India. University of California Press. Berkeley. '58.

Moraes, Frank. Jawaharlal Nehru: a biography. Macmillan. New York. '58.

Morgan, K. W. Religion of the Hindus. Ronald. New York. '53.

Nanda, B. R. Mahatma Gandhi: a biography. Beacon. Boston. '58.

Nehru, Jawaharlal. Discovery of India. Day. New York. '46.

Nehru, Jawaharlal. Independence and after. Day. New York. '50.

Nehru, Jawaharlal. Nehru visits U.S.A. Speeches during American tour 1956. Information Service of India. Washington, D.C. '57.

Nehru, Jawaharlal. Toward freedom. Day. New York. '41.

Overstreet, G. D. and Windmiller, Marshall. Communism in India. University of California Press. Berkeley. '59.

Oxford economic atlas for India and Ceylon. Oxford University Press. New York. '53.

Park, R. L. Leadership and political institutions in India. Princeton University Press. Princeton, N.J. '59.

Parton, Margaret. Leaf and the flame. Knopf. New York. '59.

Pitt, Malcolm. Introducing Hinduism. Friendship Press. New York. '55.

Rawlinson, H. G. India: a short cultural history. Praeger. New York. '52.

Seligman, Eustace. What the United States can do about India. New York University Press. New York. '56.

*Sheean, Vincent. Assignment . . . Nehru; interview, August 21, 1959. Westinghouse Broadcasting Company. 122 E. 42d St. New York 17. '59.

Sheean, Vincent. Lead kindly light. Random House. New York. '49.

Talbot, Phillips and Poplai, S. L. India and America: a study of their relations. Harper. New York. '58.

Taylor, Edmond. Richer by Asia. Houghton. Boston. '47.

*Trumbull, Robert. India since independence. (Headline series) Foreign Policy Association. New York. May-June '54.

*United States. Senate. Committee on Foreign Relations. Subcommittee on Disarmament. Control and reduction of Armaments—disarmament and security in eastern and southern Asia. (Staff Study no 9) Supt. of Docs. Washington 25, D.C. '57.

Weiner, Myron. Party politics in India. Princeton University Press. Princeton, N.J. '57.

Wint, Guy. Spotlight on Asia. Penguin Books. Baltimore. '59.

Woytinsky, W. S. India: the awakening giant. Harper. New York. '57.

Zinkin, Taya. India changes. Oxford University Press. New York. '58.

PERIODICALS

America. 101:218-19. Ap. 18, '59. Asia's Hungary.

Annals of the American Academy of Political and Social Science. 324: 56-65. Jl. '59. Propaganda battle in India and Burma, with questions and answers. F. N. Trager.

Atlantic Monthly. 199:4+. My. '57. Atlantic report: Kashmir.

Atlantic Monthly. 201:68-70. F. '58. Muslim and Hindu. F. M. Bennett.

Atlantic Monthly. 202:10+. Ag. '58. Atlantic report: communism in India.

*Atlantic Monthly. 202:77-8+. O. '58. Can India finance her five-year plan? G. L. Mehta.

*Atlantic Monthly. 203:12+. Je. '59. Atlantic report: India.

*Atlantic Monthly. 204:48-51. O. '59. India's masses. Arthur Bonner.

Business Week. p 112+. F. 8, '58. U.S. agrees to bail out India.

Business Week. p 164-5+. Ap. 18, '59. Soviets score success with Bhilai steel mill.

Catholic World. 189:432-4. S. '59. Kerala Communists face a crisis. K. K. Jacobs.

Christian Century. 76:746-8. Je. 24, '59. Toward understanding India. A. M. Stillman.

Christian Science Monitor. Je. 16, '59. Building India's future. P. M. Balasundaram.

Christian Science Monitor. p 9. O. 28, '59. India—awakening giant. H. K. Smith.

Commentary. 22:525-32. D. '56. Paradox of Jawaharlal Nehru. G. F. Hudson.

Commonweal. 54:329-31. Jl. 13, '51. New constitution for an old land. J. D. Souza.

*Congressional Record. 105:2483-7. F. 19, '59. Economic gap; speech of February 19, 1959. J. F. Kennedy.

Current History. 30:65-72. F. '56. India's outlook on foreign affairs. N. D. Palmer.

Current History. 30:104-9. F. '56. British heritage. G. T. Little.

Current History. 34:340-5. Je. '58. Kashmir and India's foreign policy. Werner Levi.

*Current History. 36:129-92. Mr. '59. India between East and West [entire issue].
Reprinted in this book: Parties and politics in India. K. M. Panikkar. p 153-7. India and the United States: maturing relations. N. D. Palmer. p 129-34.

*Economic World (Committee for International Economic Growth). 1:5. My. '59. Private foreign investment in India.

Economic World. 1:5. My. '59. U. S. Ambassador Bunker, reporting from New Delhi, cites progress, attitudes. Ellsworth Bunker.

*Economic World. 1:6. My. '59. India racing to feed 480 million by 1966.

*Economic World. 1:A1-A4. My. '59. India—United States 1959 [inserted supplement].
Reprinted in this book: External aid to India from other nations. p A-1; Silent revolution. p A-3.

Economist. 188:541-2. Ag. 16, '58. India the uncommitted.

Economist. 189:1092-3. D. 20, '58. India's disillusion with Peking.

Editorial Research Reports. 1, no 16:305-21. Ap. 29, '59. India's hard years. Lorna Marley.

Far Eastern Survey. 28:134-42. S. '59. Indian political studies and the scope of comparative politics. L. I. Rudolph and S. H. Rudolph.

Far Eastern Survey. 28:145-59. O. '59. India's food crisis. R. H. Mills, Jr.

Foreign Affairs. 28:499-501. Ap. '50. India's democratic constitution. S. R. Sharma.

Foreign Affairs. 34:432-40. Ap. '56. India's foreign policy. V. L. Pandit.

Foreign Affairs. 34:620-36. Jl. '56. Challenge to Indian nationalism: language regions. S. S. Harrison.

Foreign Affairs. 34:665-72. Jl. '56. India's new five-year plan. E. P. W. da Costa.

Foreign Affairs 35:620-30. Jl. '57. Mother India thirty years after. A. M. Rosenthal.

Foreign Affairs. 36:253-66. Ja. '58. Gandhi ten years after. F. Moraes.

Foreign Affairs. 36:587-96. Jl. '58. Rival economic theories in India. J. K. Galbraith.

Foreign Affairs. 37:117-30. O. '58. Socialistic society. W. W. Lockwood.

Foreign Affairs. 38:46-60. O. '59. For principled neutrality. J. B. Kripalani.

*Foreign Policy Bulletin. 36:93-5. Mr. 1, '57. Kashmir's far-reaching impact. A. M. Rosenthal.

Foreign Policy Bulletin. 37:11-12+. O. 1, '57. India's politics: middle course or polarization? V. M. Dean.

Foreign Policy Bulletin. 37:20-2. O. 15, '57. Should U.S. give more aid to India? N. D. Palmer.

Foreign Policy Bulletin. 37:22-4. O. 15, '57. India's economy: dead end or breakthrough? V. M. Dean.

Foreign Policy Bulletin. 37:28+. N. 1, '57. Kashmir: a tangled skein. V. M. Dean.

*Foreign Policy Bulletin. 39:29+. N. 1, '59. Communists and India. G. D. Overstreet.

*India News. 4:3. Ap. 1, '59. Policy of nonalignment serves cause of world peace; report of speech by Prime Minister Jawaharlal Nehru in Indian Parliament, March 17, 1959.

India Trade Bulletin. 10:3+. Je. '59. India's economic development— the perspective. B. K. Nehru.

*Ladies' Home Journal. 76:48-9. Ag. '59. India, the glorious gamble. Walter Lippmann.

Life. 46:36-7. Je. 1, '59. Tibet's tragedy wakes up India.

Life. 46:32-3. Je. 29, '59. India's anti-Red struggle.

Look. 22:24-30+. My. 27, '58. India 1958: freedom's last hope in Asia.

Nation. 186:527-9. Je. 1, '58. Nehru and Kashmir.
    Reply with rejoinder: 187: inside cover+. Jl. 19, '58. V. R. Bhatt.

Nation. 189:183-6. O. 3, '59. Five fingers of Tibet. Michael Brecher.

New Republic. 137:8. S. 16, '57. Communist and Communist: Kerala development.

New Republic. 138:9-11. Ja. 20; 12-15. Ja. 27, '58. India; deepening crisis. M. J. Kust.

New Republic. 140:6-7. Ap. 6, '59. India and Tibet.

New Republic. 141:10-17. Ag. 10; 20-5. Ag. 24; 11-17. S. 7, '59. India, Pakistan and the U.S. S. S. Harrison.

*New York Herald Tribune. p 24. O. 21, '59. India and U.S. food surpluses. A. T. Steele.

*New York Herald Tribune. p 18. O. 26, '59. Really hog-wild? Joseph Alsop.

New York Post. p 26. O. 2, '59. Shadows on the temple. Max Lerner.

New York Post. p 28. O. 19, '59. Is Nehru indispensable? Max Lerner.

*New York Post. p 48. O. 21, '59. Tibetan debate. Max Lerner.

New York Times. p 32. Ap. 9, '58. India's five year plan; letter to editor. John Davenport.

*New York Times. p 22. Ap. 21, '58. Aid to India supported; letter to editor. W. W. Rostow.

*New York Times. Section 10. Ja. 25, '59. India: a program in action.
    Reprinted in this book: Constitution, government and democratic ideals of India. P. N. Sapru. p 13+.

*New York Times. p 12. Ap. 28, '59. Excerpts from Nehru's statement on situation in Tibet.

New York Times. p E5. Ag. 30, '59. Nehru view of China undergoes a change. Walter H. Waggoner.

New York Times. p E4. S. 6, '59. India now questions Nehru's leadership. Robert Trumbull.

*New York Times. p 12. D. 14, '59. Eisenhower stresses freedom is more important than peace; texts of speeches at New Delhi.

*New York Times. p E3. Ja. 17, '60. Peiping action spurs India-Pakistan amity. T. J. Hamilton.

New York Times. p 1+. Ja. 26, '60. "Untied" U.S. funds sought for Indus aid. E. L. Dale, Jr.

New York Times Magazine. p 9+. N. 20, '55. Communism's no. one target in Asia. A. M. Rosenthal.

*New York Times Magazine. p 9+. F. 5, '56. India: a case history in the cold war. A. M. Rosenthal.

New York Times Magazine. p 13+. Mr. 11, '56. Nehru explains India's split personality. Jawaharlal Nehru.

New York Times Magazine. p 12+. My. 5, '57. Clouds over Kashmir. A. M. Rosenthal.

New York Times Magazine. p 9+. Ag. 11, '57. India's great adventure, ten years later. A. M. Rosenthal.

New York Times Magazine. p 25+. O. 13, '57. Questions India asks us and vice versa. A. M. Rosenthal.

New York Times Magazine. p 21+. Mr. 1, '59. India's untouchables, still the black sin. Elie Abel.

New York Times Magazine. p 18+. Ag. 16, '59. Coexistence in Kerala. Peggy Durdin.

New York Times Magazine. p 9+. S. 6, '59. New role for India's "Holy Men." R. K. Narayan.

New York Times Magazine. p 14+. S. 20, '59. Village well: drama of India. Peggy Streit and Pierre Streit.

*New York Times Magazine. p 11+. O. 4, '59. An enigma caught in a dilemma. Robert Trumbull.

New York Times Magazine. p 15+. N. 1, '59. "Most important woman in India." Paul Grimes.

Newsweek. 53:40. Mr. 2, '59. Tidal wave of humans.

Newsweek. 53:38. My. 18, '59. Nehru at close range. E. K. Lindley.

Newsweek. 54:48+. S. 21, '59. Baffled Mr. Nehru.

Pacific Affairs. 32:89-91. Mr. '59. India and military dictatorships. Taya Zinkin.

*Population Bulletin. p 153-71. D. '58. India: high cost of high fertility. R. C. Cook.

Problems of Communism. 8:27-35. Mr.-Ap. '59. Communism in India. S. S. Harrison.

Problems of Communism. 8:35-43. Mr.-Ap. '59. Communists and Indian labor. B. M. Toofan.

Reporter. 16:36-40. Mr. 21; 32-5. Ap. 4; 36-9. Ap. 18, '57. Excerpts from an Indian journal. Christine Weston.

*Reporter. 18:15-18. My. 29, '58. India's ten years of revolution by consent. William Clark.

Reporter. 19:30-3. Ag. 7, '58. Kerala: an Indian bear walks the tightrope. Seyom Brown.

Reporter. 19:29-31. S. 4, '58. Where India meets Red China high in the Himalayas. Gordon Shepherd.

Reporter. 19:29-33. O. 2, '58. India: a tale of two steel mills. Douglass Cater.

Reporter. 19:28-32. N. 13, '58. Pandit Nehru's one-party democracy. George Bailey.

Saturday Evening Post. 230:44-5+. S. 14, '57. India faces the facts of life. Cameron Hawley.
Same abridged: Reader's Digest. 71:111-16. D. '57.

*Saturday Evening Post. 232:25+. S. 19, '59. Land of too many people. Milton Silverman and Margaret Silverman.

Saturday Evening Post. 232:32-3+. O. 10, '59. In Gandhi's footsteps. Arthur Bonner.

Saturday Review. 40:7-10+. Ja. 5, '57. Dialogue on India. Chester Bowles and Earl Warren.

Senior Scholastic. 70:708. F. 8, '57. India annexes Kashmir.

Senior Scholastic. 70:9-12+. Ap. 5, '57. India, an Asian vote for democracy.

Senior Scholastic. 74:8-11. F. 13, '59. India's villages, seedbeds of democracy.

Senior Scholastic. 74:20. My. 8, '59. Farm revolution in India.

Time. 70:24+. Ag. 12, '57. Communists in office.

Time. 73:20. Mr. 2, '59. Flood of babies.

Time. 73:20. My. 4, '59. Facing starvation.

Time. 74:21. Ag. 24, '59. Precarious frontiers.

U.S. News & World Report. 40:106-9. Ja. 27, '56. What India's Nehru is really up to; conclusions of Foreign Policy Research Institute study, United States-India tensions. A. J. Cottrell and J. E. Dougherty.

U.S. News & World Report. 40:138-43. Ap. 27, '56. Reuther praises India, criticizes U.S. policy; address, April 5, 1956.

U.S. News & World Report. 41:57-60+. D. 28, '56. Nehru talks of Russia, arms race, Red China in U.N.; press conference, December 19, 1956.

U.S. News & World Report. 41:63-4. D. 28, '56. Why India is neutral; address, December 18, 1956. Jawaharlal Nehru.
  Same with title Dedicated to democratic way of life. Vital Speeches of the Day. 23:169-70. Ja. 1, '57.
U.S. News & World Report. 42:66-7. F. 8, '57. Why Nehru risks war in Kashmir.
U.S. News & World Report. 43:60-2. S. 13, '57. What's happened to Nehru?
*U.S. News & World Report. 43:68+. O. 11, '57. Where 55 million are segregated.
U.S. News & World Report. 46:49-50. Je. 29, '59. India learns about communism the hard way. J. Law.
U.S. News & World Report. 47:68-9. Ag. 3, '59. Where U.S. suddenly is popular.
*U.S. News & World Report. 47:35-8. S. 14, '59. Nehru learns about Reds . . . the hard way.
U.S. News & World Report. 47:92-3. O. 19, '59. Conquest by map: the cold war on India.
U.S. News & World Report. 47:120-3. O. 19, '59. How materialism has failed in the foreign aid program. P. C. Jain.
United States Department of State Bulletin. 36:47-50. Ja. 14, '57. Visit of Prime Minister Nehru of India.
United States Department of State Bulletin. 38:554-9. Ap. 7, '58. India and the United States work for peace; address, February 14, 1958. H. C. Lodge.
United States Department of State Bulletin. 39:856-8. D. 1, '58. Colombo plan nations hold tenth annual meeting; remarks by President Eisenhower.
Vital Speeches of the Day. 23:459-60. My. 15, '57. Parliamentary democracy; address, March 28, 1957. Jawaharlal Nehru.
*Wall Street Journal. p 12. S. 16, '57. Subsidizing socialism.
World Politics. 10:378-86. Ap. '58. Some political aspects of economic development in India. Wilfred Malenbaum.
World Today. 14:200-12. My. '58. India's planners face a crisis.
World Today. 15:236-46. Je. '59. Indian reactions to crisis in Tibet.
World Today. 15:277-86. Jl. '59. Indian Communist party today.

Date